IMPOSSIBLE GOD
GOD OF THE SKEPTIC

JUSTIN LARKIN

TABLE OF CONTENTS

SPECIAL ACKNOWLEDGMENTS

To my God: Without you, I'm lost. You saved me and
gave me a purpose. Thank you for using me.

To my wife: Fay, you're my best friend and I love
you more and more every single day. Thank you for
loving me.

To my sons: Jonas and Tobias, through you I see how
God sees all of us. Everyday I get with you is a blessing
from God.

To my editor Mike Hoornstra: Thank you for your
friendship, your encouragement and your patience.

To my dad: I love you. I miss you. I'm sorry.

INTRODUCTION

I'm not the guy who grew up in the church. I'm the guy who only went to church on special days (Christmas, Easter, funerals, Bar Mitzvah's... oops wrong religion).

I'm not the guy whose dad was a pastor. My dad was a paper boy. Not a Christian paper boy. Just a paper boy.

I'm not the guy who was raised in a Christian household. I wasn't even raised in "a" household. My parents were divorced when I was three years old. I was raised in "households."

I'm not the guy who has been a Christian for as long as he can remember. I'm the guy that at age twenty, drank way too much alcohol (I did this many times) and woke up on a friend's floor with no idea how I got there or where my pants were. After a fruitless search for my pants, I settled on a pair of basketball shorts— they weren't mine. I walked to the the middle of the University of South Florida campus to meet with a campus pastor.

My life changed that day. I was introduced to God by a genuine follower of Christ. Shortly after that meeting, I was baptized and my journey with God began. I went from a complete skeptic to a genuine follower of Christ.

I want to introduce you to the same God that I met years ago. He changed my life and I know that he can change yours too.

P.S. I tend to go off on tangents. Pretty much like I'm doing right now. So instead of putting all of them into the body of this book, I used my endnotes to explore my tangents. Read them if you want, or don't.

Chapter 1

IRRATIONAL, ILLOGICAL, AND IMPOSSIBLE

"Our duty is found in the revealed will of God in the Scriptures. Our trust must be in the sovereign will of God as He works in the ordinary circumstances of our daily lives for our good and His glory."　　　　　—Jerry Bridges

I was sitting in a Starbucks sipping a Venti Pike Place Roast coffee and writing. Everyone knows that Starbucks is the place to go to unravel the mysteries of God and I was in one of those moods. I asked myself "What does it mean to be God?" Then I stopped and thought, "I can't just jump into this, I have start somewhere else," so I changed the question. "What does it mean to be Justin?" No way, that's just too personal and quite honestly, that list would freak some people out. Let's go with "What does it mean to be a man?" Yeah, let's start with that. So I sent a text message out to those whom, at the time, I thought were men. I then realized that I was mistaken when I got certain responses from certain men that I no longer consider men.[1] Of the men remaining on my list, this is what we came up with in response to the question. I must warn you that this is the shallow version of the Man List, and there are, of course, some exceptions that I will point out along the way. Anyway, this is what it means to be a man.

What Does It Mean To Be A Man: The Shallow Version

- You didn't cry when you watched the Titanic-because you didn't *watch* the Titanic. That goes for The Notebook as well.

- You did, however, tear up when you saw the first Transformers movie and Bumblebee was injured so badly that you didn't know if he was going to make it or not.

- Your idea of a manicure is just biting your nails off; the same thing for a pedicure.

- You can bench more than 95 lbs.[2]

- You believe that Will Ferrell has been overlooked for an Academy Award every year. You're such a fan that you would be willing to give him a kidney even if he didn't ask.

- You consider Texas De Brazil the pinnacle of culinary greatness.

- You can't spell… and you don't care.[3]

- You never wear skinny jeans. Wearing pants should never cut off your air supply.[4]

- You're wearing a shirt that just barely passed the sniff test: "Uh, not that bad."

- Your body is covered in hair.[5]

- You're willing and able to fight a grizzly bear and win. Or you just look like a grizzly bear with your shirt off.

- You go golfing to relax when you're stressed out and you come back more stressed out than before.[6]

- You can grow a beard. Not one like Joe Dirt... a full beard.

- If your mom was hospitalized during the Super Bowl, you would give her a call during halftime. [7]

- Wrestling is real! If you say it's fake, then my friend that weighs 125 lbs would be more than willing to RKO you and show you otherwise![8]

There you go- what it means to be a man. I am only qualified to speak on behalf of the men. Ladies, you're responsible for your own list. According to my wife, being a fan of "Grey's Anatomy" and "washing your hands before handling food" would be somewhere on that list. Anyway, I had to do this before I tackled the question of what it means to be God.

50 Reasons Why God Is Imaginary

Normally, when you talk about describing God, you typically go into **God's "Omni" Attributes.** Basically, it would go like this: God is omnipresent, omniscient, omnipotent, and omnibenevolent. Translated into terms that everyone can understand, it goes like this: God is all-present, all-knowing, all-powerful, and all-loving. Yes, these are all correct. We see throughout scripture these attributes of God:

> "For God is greater than our hearts, and he knows everything."[9]

> "Where can I go from your Spirit? Where can I flee from your presence? If I go up to the Heavens, you are there; if I make my bed in the depths, you are there."[10]

> "Ah, Sovereign Lord, you have made the heavens and the earth by your great power and outstretched arm. Nothing is too hard for you."[11]

Understand that I went to bible college[12] and this is how you describe God. That's what my professors told me, so it has to be true... and yes, it is true. However, what it means to be God actually came alive to me not in a bible college course but rather in the writings of an atheist. I would like to take the time to thank that atheist (skeptic, non-believer, whatever he likes to be called). I found that his very reason for God not existing is actually my definition of what it means to be God. So, thank you very much for making this clear and evident to me.

I came across this blog that was completely focused on proving that God is imaginary. Honestly, I was pretty impressed with the blog because it had a list of **50 Proofs Why God Is Imaginary**. That's kind of impressive- 50 proofs! So I read a few of them and this individual sure did his research. You can tell he spent a lot of time on this blog. But the truth is that even with all that time he spent on disproving God, he missed the point. Actually, he provided me with a very profound definition of what it means to be God.

He started by talking about the miracles of Jesus and how the lack of evidence of his healing people and turning water into wine proved that it didn't happen. He says that you cannot prove the turning of water into wine and the healings through a scientific study. Here's what he says:

"Neither of these miracles can be scientifically tested today. Not one of Jesus' miracles left any tangible evidence for scientists to study."[13]

And guess what? I can't argue with that. He's right. there is nothing scientific for us to study. You've got me on that one, "Mr. Imaginary" (That's what I call him, because it's fun). I kept reading and that's when it jumped out at me. Because of the lack of evidence to scientifically prove Jesus' miracles, Mr. Imaginary says this:

"For any normal, rational person, the reason is obvious— God is imaginary."[14]

There it was, and it was beautiful- the attempt to rationalize God. Well, I have news for you. God is *not* rational. God is *not* logical. God is *not* normal. That is what makes God God and not you or me. It's the irrational, the illogical, the **impossible**. God is God and we are not. That's the problem: we try to make God like us. That is what rationalizing God attempts to do, but guess what? We can't rationalize Him. It is impossible, because God is Impossible. **That's what makes him God.**

"**God**" is the fourth word in the Bible. It translates from the word elohiym. A word that is plural in form but singular in meaning and its main focus is great power. It means "person" characterized by greatness and power: mighty one, great one, judge. Let's get away from the Hebrew and just take a look at how good ole Webster defines "God". Webster says: **the Being perfect in power, wisdom, and goodness who is worshipped as creator and ruler of the universe.** Thank you very much, Webster. What does it mean to be God? The very definition means *to be impossible*. There is your definition- what does it mean to be God...

It means to be impossible

"Baby Making Time!"

When look at how scripture describes Jesus, we see that he is both 100% man and 100% God. According to all ration and logic this is impossible. God is also God the Father, God the Son, and God the Spirit... all three in one. Once again, impossible. Look at his time on earth and all that he did in his public ministry. Every single miracle that he performs make no sense. It is not normal.

It is impossible. But it all started with a young teenage girl named Mary.

When my wife told me that she was pregnant, my response was not the best. I just sat there and stared blankly at the wall for about 30 minutes. Not one of my finest moments. You might be thinking to yourself: "Oh, an unplanned pregnancy?" No, we planned. We did a lot of planning. Our plan was to wait at least five years into our marriage before we had kids, and that's what we did. Our first child was so planned that I actually scheduled it in my iCalendar: "Time to make a baby!" However, no amount of planning could have prepared my 30-year-old ears to hear those words: "I'm pregnant, we're going to have a baby".

"Violent and Bloody"

When people announce the arrival of a child, it sounds very pleasant. "We're having a baby." That's not what's going to happen at all. You should say "We're going to war." That's more accurate.

I became a Christian when I was twenty years old. The guy who shared the gospel with me and eventually baptized me was thirty and getting ready to have his first child. I remember his first words to me afterwards: "childbirth is violent and bloody." He was exactly right. My wife had a c-section and I got to watch as my son entered the world. He entered the world via what looked like a giant metal shoehorn prying open my wife's stomach and a nurse dropping atomic elbows into her abdomen in hopes of squeezing my little boy out. All the while, the anesthesiologist was yelling "Breath and bend your knees so you don't pass out." I yelled back "I AM!" My wife was thoroughly drugged laying on the table saying things like "We should buy a boat!"

At the birth of my second son, my wife had another c-section. I remember thinking, "I made it through the first one, I know what to expect." I stood up and looked just as they were cutting into my wife's abdomen. Blood shot everywhere and I quietly sat back down in utter shock. That's what child birth is like. It's like going to war. Those images are burned into my mind forever. Childbirth is violent and bloody.

Now that we're on the same page, I want you to think about a teenage girl hearing those words, "Surprise, you're pregnant!" The mind of a teenage girl is not prepared to deal with the reality of those words. A teenage girl does not know what to do with this type of information.

Eleven Years Ago...

There was a family in my church that had a thirteen year old daughter. The family was excited about coming to church. Everyone except the daughter, that is. I was a young minister, so I internalized everything and took this young lady's lack of interest in youth group as a personal attack on me. What can I say? I was very self-conscious.

One day I got a call. The young lady had just been arrested for abandoning her baby. What? I had no idea she was even pregnant. The truth was that nobody else did either. She was secretly dating an 18-year-old boy. When she found out she was pregnant, she wrapped an Ace bandage around her waist to keep her stomach from showing and started wearing baggy cloths. She did this for the entire pregnancy: No one noticed.

Then one night while her parents were at work and she was all alone, she gave birth to a baby girl in the bathroom of her apartment. Then she did the unthinkable. She wrapped the baby up in a blanket, carefully placed the baby in the trashcan, and took the trash out. About thirty minutes later, a neighbor was taking out their garbage when they heard the baby crying. They saved the baby and immediately dialed 911. The baby survived.

Our first response when we heard this was shock and disgust. How could she do such a thing? But the truth was that her mind wasn't prepared for everything that she went through. She was thirteen and going through the pain and agony alone in a bathroom.

Eleven years ago I was sitting in a courtroom looking at a teenage girl in an orange jumpsuit appearing before the judge and I thought to myself, "The mind of a teenage girl is not prepared to deal with the reality of having a baby." She was alone, confused, scared and in excruciating pain. Now, 2000 years ago, imagine Mary's surprise when God told her that she was pregnant with the Son of God.

God sent his angel Gabriel with an impossible message to Mary. The text is found beginning in **Luke 1:26**:

In the sixth month, God sent the angel Gabriel to Nazareth, a town in Galilee, to a virgin pledged to be married to a man named Joseph, a descendant of David. The virgin's name was Mary.

"Virgin?"

Okay, I don't really think I need to explain this, but on the off chance that someone is reading this book that has no idea what a "virgin" is, let me explain. According to medical dictionaries, a virgin is "one who has the quality or condition of being a virgin; one who is in the state of being a virgin." What? That makes no sense whatsoever. That is a horrible definition of a virgin. "Condition?" This definition makes a virgin sound like a disease or a rash. Can you imagine your doctor giving this diagnosis: "I have some bad news sir. You're a virgin, you're not going to make it." Let's try this again. According to a different source, a virgin is "being used or worked for the fir...." AHHHHHH! You have got to be kidding me! That's what I get for Googling 'definition of virgin.' Need a different approach. What would dad say? Nevermind, that definitely won't work either. Dad's definition scarred me for life. Why don't I just give you my definition?

A virgin is someone who has not yet had sex. You know, "intercourse," "going all the way," "the horizontal mambo" or "the vertical mambo," "bow-chick-a-wow-wow," "boomtangle" (thank you Urban Dictionary for that one). A virgin is a person that has never had sex and no a virgin is not a myth. It is a person who saved their virginity as symbol of purity and respect.

Mary the Virgin

In **verse 27**, Luke doesn't waste any time telling us that Mary was a virgin. It's central to the story. In those days, a young woman would be betrothed to a man almost immediately after puberty (obviously they knew something about the teenage hormone problem back then too).

Mary may have just entered her teens. The betrothal was a legally binding relationship, but intercourse was not permitted until marriage. Mary was betrothed to a man named Joseph.

This is when the angel Gabriel showed up and said "Greetings, you who are highly favored! The Lord is with you." Now, Luke said that Mary was "greatly troubled" by Gabriel's greeting. Why would Mary have a hard time with what he said to her? You don't see too many people looking too much into this verse, but I believe it gives us a look into the character of Mary. We know that Mary was a virgin, telling us that she was a young woman of purity. I think this exchange shows that Mary was a young woman of God who was very humble as well. Not to mention that there was more of a fear of God back in those days that we have seemingly lost in our society. So Mary was "greatly troubled," or in our words, she was "freaking out."

Gabriel saw how troubled she was and comforted her with these words in **verse 30**... "Do not be afraid, Mary, you have found favor with God." The word here for 'favor' is translated from the greek word "charis" which is the same word for 'grace.' Mary has received the grace of God, or in other words, "she has received the undeserved favor of God." That had to make Mary feel better. I can imagine Mary exhaling as she heard these words. "Boy do I feel better."

Now I happen to think that Gabriel was a master communicator. He saw that she was freaking out and he eased her emotions only to deliver the most shocking news ever.

But the angel said to her, "Do not be afraid, Mary, you have found favor with God. You will be with child and give birth to a son, and you are to give him the name Jesus. He will be great and will be called the Son of the Most High. The Lord God will give him the throne of his father David, and he will reign over the house of Jacob forever; his kingdom will never end."[15]

And there you have it, Master Communicator Gabriel. **"MARY YOU HAVE RECEIVED THE FAVOR OF GOD**... by the way, your pregnant." WHAT?!! This is more than just shocking news, it's impossible. Mary states the obvious, "How will this be," Mary asked the angel, "since I am a virgin?" Good question, Mary. That's exactly what every single one of us would say.

Parthenogenesis?

So, is a virgin birth possible? Parthenogenesis is a word that is from the combination of the Greek words *parthenos*, "virgin" and *genesis*, "birth." This is the study of asexual reproduction found in females, where growth and development of embryos occurs without fertilization by a male. Now, I'm no doctor, nor do I play one on TV (that would be cool though), but we do see asexual reproduction in nature. We see it in plants. It's also seen in invertebrate animal species like water fleas, some bees, some scorpion species and certain kinds of wasp. But it also occurs in some vertebrates. Some reptiles, fish, and very rarely in birds and sharks. But it does happen. So the answer is yes.

But is this possible in humans? Can an embryo grow and develop without the fertilization of the male chromosomes? No. Theoretically it could happen, but one thing about parthenogenesis is that when it comes to the XY chromosome sex determination, when there is not male fertilization then the offspring will always be female. But there is no scientific evidence to support that partheno-genesis can happen in humans... it's impossible.

Mary knew this was impossible which led to her questioning Gabriel. His response went like this...

> The angel answered, "The Holy Spirit will come upon you, and the power of the Most High will overshadow you. So the holy one to be born will be called the Son of God.

> Even Elizabeth your relative is going to have a child in her old age, and she who was said to be barren is in her sixth month. <u>For nothing is impossible with God</u>."[16]

And there you have it, something that is impossible for the smartest scientist of our time is simply explained as the power of the Holy Spirit. We have to understand that we are talking about the God that spoke the world into existence.

This book will talk about the God that opens his mouth, speaks, and brings the world into existence. The world that you and I are living on. The earth beneath our feet didn't exist until God said so. This book will talk about Jesus- All God, All Man doing the impossible for those in need. With a touch, a man can see. With a wave of his hand, a raging storm in the open ocean is silenced. With just his presence, demons tremble and beg for mercy. With a single word, "rise", a dead girl will breath again. This book will talk about a journey to unravel the impossible knot of sin that we have worked our way into. A knot that only his pure love can remove from our lives but only on a deadly cross. This book will talk about the God that takes the full blast of his own wrath on himself so that we could be with him.

"How will you respond?"

The baby in Mary's belly didn't exist until God said so. The power of the Holy Spirit moves- and there you have it- a baby in a virgin. And Gabriel removes every single one of our questions with one simple sentence that will serve as the inspiration of this book and also our lives.

"For nothing is impossible with God."

The only question is, how will you respond? Will you run away with your rational and logical thinking? Will you close this book, never to open it again, then shut yourself in your room and cry yourself to sleep because you just can't figure it all out? Or, will you respond like Mary did... "I am the Lord's servant," Mary answered. "May it be to me as you have said."? Will you embrace the irrational? Will you embrace the illogical? Will you embrace the impossible and all the implications that it has on the way you live each moment of your life and how you follow Him? How you respond determines where we go from here. If you can't take it, then close this book now. If you're ready to embrace the impossible one, then turn the page.

What Do You Think?

1. Take a moment to write out the omni- attributes of God. If God possesses these attributes, should

it encourage or discourage our trust in him? Why do you think that is so?

2. Everything about God defies our logic. Our reasoning says that everything about God is impossible, but that's what makes Him God and not man like us. God specializes in the impossible, how does that affect your family, your job, your friendships, your marriage, etc.?

3. Read Jeremiah 32:26-27. God speaks very boldly and confidently about who He is and all that He can accomplish. How does that make you feel? Are you comforted? Are you frightened? Are you excited?

Chapter 2

"BEE BEE YOU!!!"

"The soul can do without everything except the word of God, without which none at all of its wants are provided for."   –Martin Luther

Well if you're reading these words it means you aren't cowering in your room afraid to embrace the impossible. Or it means that you just finished cowering in your room and now you're ready to embrace the impossible. Whatever the case, good to have you back. Let's get to work.

Our words are very powerful. What verbally comes out of our mouths is very important. There is a reason why scripture speaks about being careful with our tongues.

"If anyone considers himself religious and yet does not keep a tight rein on his tongue, he deceives himself and his religion is worthless." [17]

"Whoever would love life and see good days must keep his tongue from evil and his lips from deceitful speech."[18]

Paul gives us this warning... "Let your conversation be always full of grace, seasoned with salt, so that you may know how to answer everyone." [19]

We take for granted how powerful our conversations can be. How people respond to us depends highly on what we say. One funny word will make someone laugh. One mean word and they could be crying. One soft word can melt the hardest of hearts. One harsh word and you can find yourself in a fight. One rude word and you might lose a friendship. On the other side, one gentle word and you might have a new friend. Our words are very powerful and can change lives.

Something else that I have come to realize about the power of words is that sometimes it depends on who is saying them. Think about that for a second. There is a difference between your boss saying "Great job on that presentation Marvin!" and your wife saying it. You can't help but think, "My wife has to say that!" It depends on who's saying the words. When I have to go out of the country on a mission trip, it's different when my wife says "I'll miss you!" than when my music minister says it. It's extremely different and creepy.

When one of my kids looks at me and goes "Dad, I love you!" it means more to me than if anyone else says it. When my younger son holds his plastic golf club like it's a gun, points it at my face and yells "BEE BEE YOU! BEE BEE YOU!" ("Bee Bee You" is the sound he makes for a gun. If it's a small gun then it's a high pitch "BEE

BEE YOU!" Bigger guns call for a deeper "BEE BEE YOU!"). When my son says that, it's cute. If my youth minister says it, I start to fear for my life.

Words are powerful, but whoever speaks those words has the potential to change everything.

"What Are We Waiting For!"

I remember as a young minister having talks with my mom about God. My mom would go to church regularly but never entered into the waters of baptism to start her relationship with God. I had countless conversations with her trying to get her to understand how she needs to respond. I thoroughly explained why and how according to scripture. I was working hard, but every single time my mom would just brush me off. She would actually kind of laugh me off: "silly boy!"[20]

Then one night one of my professors from college was at the church teaching a class. The next thing I know, everyone was filing into the auditorium. Someone turned to me and said "Your mom's getting baptized!" Now I have to admit that my response was not the best. I said "Why?" Not the best response to your mom getting baptized. I said "why" and someone replied, "Professor Bundy said to the class 'you need to be baptized' and your mom stood up and said 'what are we waiting for?'"

Well, I can't really blame her. I pretty much did the same thing. For as long as I can remember people would say to me "you know Jesus died for your sins." Of course, I would just brush it off and go on with my life. Then one day I was at the University of South Florida having coffee with a campus minister. He said "So, Tampa Bay's having a pretty good season." I said, "They are having a good season." Then he said "You know, Jesus died for your sins." I replied "Really, tell me more." The next thing you know I'm getting baptized.

"The Bull" Donald Prickett

Words in themselves are very powerful, but whoever says those words has the potential to change everything. I want you to take a few moments and think about a person in your life right now that you respect. When that person speaks, you pay special attention. When they speak up, you know that you need to listen.

The person that I always pay special attention to is Donald Prickett. When Donald and I worked together in youth ministry, I nicknamed him "the Bull." It sounded really cool and all the kids loved it. We would be sitting around in discussion and all of a sudden Donald would speak up out of nowhere. It would be very profound and insightful. I would think to myself: "Where did that come from?" Ever since then, I learned to pay special attention whenever he spoke up. To this day, we will be in leadership meeting and I will just stare at Donald waiting for him to say something profound and insightful. It creeps him out, but I do it anyway.

Words are very powerful, but whoever speaks those words has the potential to transform. So when God speaks, you can expect the impossible.

"In The Beginning..."

Our God defies human logic. He specializes in doing the impossible. Nothing speaks to this more than the creation story.

"In the beginning, God created the heavens and the earth. The earth was without form and void, and darkness was over the face of the deep. And the Spirit of God was hovering over the face of the waters."[21]

The word "create" means to "form or shape." How does God "form or shape" the heaven and the earth? And God said, "Let there be light," and there was light. Notice the connection between "God created" and "God said." The voice of God was the means by which creation was sparked. Nothing existed until God said so. The earth was nothing until God said so. By his voice, life was breathed into this world. It started with light breaking the darkness. He didn't stop there, he spoke and land rose from the depths of the sea. He said the word and trees and plants started to grow. His voice threw the stars into the night sky. His voice brought to life all kinds of different creatures. He's not finished yet. With his voice, man and woman were created. By the time God was done speaking all of creation into existence, he looked at all he had done and said "looking good!"

"If God Doesn't..."

Go ahead and attempt to wrap your mind around that for a few moments. If God doesn't say so then there is no light to see. Wherever you are right now, if you can, turn the lights out and just sit there for a second. This is your world if God doesn't speak. Go ahead and turn the lights back on, because you can't read if you can't see. Go ahead and pick your right foot up. Now put it back down. Feel that? It's the ground. If God doesn't say so, then none of that exists. There is no earth beneath your feet. Go home and pet your dog Sparky. Tap on the glass of your aquarium and watch your goldfish freak out (Let's be honest, goldfish look freaked out or surprised all of the time. Every time I see a goldfish, I thank God for giving me eyelids). If God didn't say so, they don't exist.

Go ahead and stand up. If in the beginning God didn't speak man into existence, you couldn't stand up right now. Clap your hands together. If in the beginning God didn't speak man into existence, you couldn't clap right now. Put your hands up in the air and wave them side to side. Now yell out "BEE BEE YOU, BEE BEE YOU!"

(Dramatic Pause)

Okay, I just wanted to see if I could get you to do that. Sit down, you look ridiculous. The point is, if in the beginning God hadn't spoken man into existence, you couldn't do what you just did right now. Let that humble you.

Our words are powerful, but only God's word can do the impossible. That's exactly what you and I want. That's exactly what you and I need. Therefore, when God speaks, you need to listen because his words have the power to change your life.

Elijah's Depression

In **1 Kings 19** we see the aftermath of the showdown at Mount Caramel. The prophet of God, Elijah, had just finished making fools of King Ahab and his 450 prophets of Baal. From our perspective, the odds were against Elijah, 450 to 1. Those seem like impossible odds. Well what Ahab and his prophets didn't take into account was the one true God working through Elijah. That's exactly what God did. God and Elijah made fools out of the false prophets.

When you get to **chapter 19,** you see that King Ahab and Queen Jezebel were furious about being upstaged by Elijah. A price was put out on Elijah's life and he went into hiding. He ran for his life. He left every one behind and hid in the woods. Look at verse 3...

> "Elijah was afraid[a] and ran for his life. When he came to Beersheba in Judah, he left his servant there, while he himself went a day's journey into the wilderness. He came to a broom bush, sat down under it and prayed that he might die. "I have had enough, Lord," he said. "Take my life; I am no better than my ancestors." Then he lay down under the bush and fell asleep."[22]

Beersheba is about 80 miles south of Jezreel, so Elijah was booking it without letting up a single bit. When he finally got there, he was all alone and sitting under a tree. It says that he prayed for death, Elijah was pretty depressed. Understandably so. The results at Mount Caramel probably weren't what Elijah was expecting. He was more than likely expecting mass repentance of the entire country. Instead, it only resulted in a death threat. God fed Elijah and after he recovered his strength he got up and started running again. This time for forty days and forty nights to mount Horeb, also known as Mount Sinai.

So Elijah ran. He ran all the way to Mount Sinai, where God gave Moses the ten commandments. Spurgeon writes:

"Elijah failed in the very point at which he was strongest, and that is where most men fail. In Scripture, it is the wisest man who proves himself to be the greatest fool; just as the meekest man, Moses, spoke hasty and bitter words. Abraham failed in his faith, and Job in his patience; so, he who was the most courageous of all men, fled from an angry woman."[23]

Elijah ran, failing at the one thing he was known for-his courage. He would get it back and he would get it back at Mount Sinai. Here is where God spoke to the broken Elijah.

The Gentle Voice Comforts Us

Elijah ran to Mount Sinai and spent the night in a cave... "There he went into a cave and spent the night. And the word of the Lord came to him: "What are you doing here, Elijah?"[24]

The first thing you learn is that God's word comforts us. That's what happened with Elijah. It had been over forty days, he was tired, he was depressed and he was alone. You know how that feels. Have you ever felt abandoned and alone? How many of you have found yourself struggling to get out of bed in the morning? You just lay there thinking to yourself, "not another day." We've all been there.

But what happens when your phone rings and on the other end is a kind voice saying "where have you been?" It's in those words that you say to yourself, "Someone cares. Someone loves me. I'm not forgotten."

When God asked Elijah, "What are you doing here?" He acknowledged Elijah. He told Elijah, "I see you and I haven't forgotten about you." The acknowledgement served as a comfort for a man that was completely broken.

God hasn't forgotten about you either. **1 Timothy 3:16** says that all scripture is "God-breathed," meaning that everything found in the Bible is his words. When you study his word, it communicates comfort to you over and over again.

In Paul's second letter to the Corinthian church he starts off with a reminder... "Praise be to the God and Father of our Lord Jesus Christ, the Father of compassion and the God of all comfort, who comforts us in all our troubles"[25]

The "all" in that verse translates as "individually, everything and all things." His comfort is for every individual area of your life that you struggle with. If you look back into **Romans 15:4,** you will see Paul saying that all the words written from the past were written "so that through the endurance taught in the Scriptures and the encouragement they provide we might have hope."

The psalmist writes... "The Lord is close to the brokenhearted and saves those who are crushed in spirit."[26] God inspired men to write these word down to comfort you, to remind you that he see you and that you are never alone just as the gentle voice reminded Elijah.

The Gentle Voice Guides Us

The gentle voice of God doesn't just comfort you, it also leads you. When God reached out to Elijah he asked him, "what are you doing here?" Elijah responded with an outpouring of his heart... "I have been very zealous for the Lord God Almighty. The Israelites have rejected your covenant, torn down your altars, and put your prophets to death with the sword. I am the only one left, and now they are trying to kill me too."[27]

This is the second time that God asked the same question and this is the second time that Elijah had responded in the exact same way. God was trying to get Elijah to move while Elijah just wanted to sit and wallow in what he saw as his failure. Notice that God didn't leave him there. God spokes again and gives him direction for his life, **verse 15** "Go back the way you came." God is saying, "This isn't where you're supposed to be." Many of us aren't where we are supposed to be either. How many of you wake up in the morning and say to yourself, "Why am I even here?" You would be surprised at how many people actually say those exact words.

The good news is that God's word guides us as well. When he speaks, it's a good idea to listen. When the psalmist writes "Your word is a lamp to my feet and a light for my path" he is speaking to the reality that God's word's leads us. That's the reason why so many of us struggle with where we are right now in our lives. We aren't listening to him. We aren't letting his gentle voice light our path.

Peter writes in **2 Peter 1:19**... "And we have the word of the prophets...". The prophets were the mouthpiece of God. He gave them the message and they shared it. "... made more certain, and you will do well to pay attention to it, as to a light shining in a dark place, until the day dawns and the morning star rises in your hearts." It's God's gentle voice that guides us through our life.

"Get up already!"

The last thing we see in this exchange between God and Elijah is a restoration to the man that Elijah once was. When God told him to "go back the way you came" it didn't just serve as guidance, it gave him the courage to get back up. Think about it for a second, God comforted Elijah by acknowledging him. Then God guided him back to the path he used to be on. Then he sent him with a purpose.

"Go back the way you came, and go to the Desert of Damascus. When you get there, anoint Hazael king over Aram. Also, anoint Jehu son of Nimshi king over Israel, and anoint Elisha son of Shaphat from Abel Meholah to succeed you as prophet. Jehu will put to death any who escape the sword of Hazael, and Elisha will put to death any who escape the sword of Jehu. Yet I reserve seven thousand in Israel—all whose knees have not bowed down to Baal and whose mouths have not kissed him."[28]

Let me paraphrase that for you: "Elijah, your job isn't done! Get up! Go back the way you came and finish the job I gave you. Be the man I created you to be!"

The Byproduct of Hope

The byproduct of comfort will always be hope. The byproduct of direction in life is the same thing- hope. The byproduct of hope will always be courage. Hope is what gets you out of bed in the morning. Hope is what makes you stand tall in the face of adversity. Hope is what makes you take that next tentative step. The byproduct of hope will always be courage.

Elijah was known as a man of courage. Through the struggle and trials of life he lost what he was known for. But at the cave of a mountain, in the gentle whisper of God, he found his courage again and finished the work God intended for him.

"What if God doesn't speak?"

Let's say that God didn't speak to Elijah. Let's say that God left Elijah laying in a cave on the side of a mountain. What happens to Elijah? Chances are that the grief he was experiencing would have eventually taken his life. He was tired. He was defeated. He was alone in the middle of nowhere. It was bound to happen, Elijah would have died. But that day, God didn't stay silent. He spoke and comforted a broken man. He spoke and led a lost soul. He spoke and gave courage back to a scared man. But the words of God did more than that.

In the gospel of John, we have an argument between Jesus and some of the Jewish believers. They wanted to believe in Jesus but they were struggling with some of the stuff that he was saying. Jesus was trying to get them to see their bondage in sin and the Jews were stuck on their ancestry. Jesus was saying some difficult things like "you're all slaves." The Jews replied, "No we're not. We're descendants of Abraham." Jesus would say "your father is the devil, the father of lies." The Jews went right back to "Abraham!"

Then in **John 8:47** Jesus says... "He who is of God hears the words of God; for this reason you do not hear them, because you are not of God." They, of course, argue

35

with Jesus some more. Then finally Jesus says "Truly, truly, I say to you, if anyone keeps My word he will never see death."

His gentle voice speaks and we are comforted. His gentle voice speaks and we are given direction. His gentle voice speaks and we receive courage. The gentle voice of the God that defies our logic does the impossible and saves.

What Do You Think?

1. Who do you have in your life that you pay special attention to when they speak? How is this person different from other people in your life?
2. In the creation story (Genesis 1), God spoke creation into existence. How does the formless earth specifically respond to the voice of God?
3. How does the creation story affect how you see God?
4. If the byproduct of comfort and direction is hope, how does this translate into courage?
5. Read John 8:51. What do you think Jesus meant when he said this?
6. How does this affect every area of your life?

Chapter 3

"WOULD MILK SHOOT OUT OF JESUS' NOSE?"

"The primary source of the appeal of Christianity was Jesus–His incarnation, His life, His crucifixion, and His resurrection." –Kenneth Scott Latourette

"Things I Can't Do"

What are some things that are physically impossible for you to do? Take some time and make a list of the things you cannot accomplish.

I came up with a few things that I can't do. These are things that are impossible for me to do. First of all, I can't lick my own elbow. Either elbow- it doesn't matter. I've tried many times. I just can't do it.

Nor can I roll one finger forward while rolling the other finger backwards. Its kind of like when you try to force two magnets together with the same polarity, it just doesn't work.

I cannot sneeze with my eyes open. I don't think anyone can do that, nor should they want to. I'm afraid that if I sneeze with my eyes open they will pop out of my head.

Something else that is impossible for me to do is algebra. There is just something about mixing numbers and letters together that gives me a headache. Algebra in High School was more like a dream to me. Everything is really foggy. I'm not too sure it really happened.

I cannot bench press 280 lbs. I can bench press 275 lbs., but 280 is out of the question.

I cannot tickle myself. I mean I can tickle myself, but it doesn't work. I don't even know why I know that.

I cannot stop sweating. It's in my genetics. My dad couldn't stop sweating. I can't stop sweating. My two sons are the same way. I sweat doing the most inactive things. I sweat walking from the couch to the refrigerator. I sweat watching TV. I sweat in my sleep. When I wake up in the morning, it looks like I just ran a marathon in my sleep.

These are things that are impossible for me to do. These are acts I am unable to accomplish. I know this may be hard for some of you to believe but it is true. I know I could come up with more- a lot more. Unfortunately, my ego can't take it.

"I Struggle With Jesus"

Now here's the deal- we are going to talk about a difficult belief that we must come to grips with. It has to do with who exactly Jesus is. I love Jesus more than anything. But sometimes I have a hard time describing

Jesus. I know that sounds like a confession of sorts, but hear me out.

In William Shakespeare's play *The Merchants of Venice* the play's main character is Antonio the Merchant. This is made explicit by the title page of the first section: *"The most excellent History of the Merchant of Venice."* However, the play is best known for the dramatic speech made by the play's antagonist, Shylock the Jew. Shylock is a Jewish moneylender and traditionally has been accepted as the play's villain. Many modern day readers and theatergoers see him more of a sympathetic character due to his famous speech:

> Hath not a Jew eyes? Hath not a Jew hands, organs, dimensions, senses, affections, passions; fed with the same food, hurt with the same weapons, subject to the same diseases, heal'd by the same means, warm'd and cool'd by the same winter and summer as a Christian is? If you prick us, do we not bleed? If you tickle us, do we not laugh? If you poison us, do we not die? And if you wrong us, shall we not revenge? If we are like you in the rest, we will resemble you in that. If a Jew wrong a Christian, what is his humility? Revenge. If a Christian wrong a Jew, what should his sufferance be by Christian example? Why, revenge. The villainy you teach me, I will execute, and it shall go hard but I will better the instruction.

If you're like me, the line "If you prick us, do we not bleed?" immediately catches your attention. Why is that? Because it's true. That and it's extremely quotable, so you know you've heard it somewhere else and you feel cultured because of it. But mainly because it's true. We can look different. We can sound different. We can act different. We can believe differently. But we all bleed the same.

Jesus is Just Like Us

Every time I hear this quote I can't help but think of Jesus. On one hand, Jesus is just like you or me. I've put a lot of thought into this and I am convinced that Jesus would enjoy a good slice of pizza when he's hungry. I am convinced that at the end of a long work day, he would look forward to coming home and collapsing into his favorite La-Z-Boy. Of course, he would be tired, so I am convinced he definitely would sleep and he would probably even snore when he's really exhausted. I am convinced that if you told him something funny while he was taking a drink, more than likely that drink would shoot out his nose just like it would any one of us. I am convinced that if he doesn't see that bump in the sidewalk, he would trip and scrape his knee. He would bleed just like you or I.[29] I am convinced that Jesus is just like us in many different ways.

Jesus is Nothing Like Us

On the other hand he's nothing like us. He changes water into wine. He feeds thousands with just a fish and some bread. He walks on water. He gives sight to the blind with dirt and his spit. He purifies the unclean skin of the leper. He tells a cripple man to get up and walk and he does. He even breathes new life into the dead.

I know this is hard to believe, but you have to come to grip with this belief. How can God be 100 percent God and 100 percent man at the same time? I found a website where kids were asked this question. Candice, age 10, explain it this way *"He did things like his Dad (100 percent God) and he did things like we do (since he's 100 percent man)."*[30] You would be amazed at what you can learn from kids. I think little Candice is right on because that's what we see in Scripture. Paul says "Beyond all question, the mystery from which true godliness springs is great."[31] How God actually accomplished two natures in one body is a mystery, but you cannot deny the reference in Scripture.

The clearest passage of Scripture concerning the two natures of Jesus comes from **John 1:1... In the beginning was the Word, and the Word was with God, and the Word was God.** "The Word" is referring to Jesus and it tells us two very important things about him. From the very beginning, Jesus was "with God" and he "was God." In **verse 14** you see that the Word (Jesus) takes on human flesh. God and man united in one person. Two natures, one person.

Now it's easy to say, but difficult to understand. This is what I struggle with: How can the common and uncommon co-exist? This is the type of thing that makes my head hurt. It's a mystery how the two are combined, but Jesus does it. And there is only one way for me to describe this... impossible. He accomplishes the impossible. Jesus is impossible. And this can happen because you understand that "nothing is impossible with God." You have to come to grips with this. Your belief in God is vital to your relationship with him. He wants you to believe. **God wants you to belief the unbelievable.**

The big question isn't really how. The bigger question is why do the common and the uncommon co-exist? Why is Jesus just like us and nothing like us at the same time? It's so we would believe the unbelievable.

"Let's Get Drunk And Go Bowling"

For the first six months of my new life in Christ I locked myself in my room and read my Bible. All my friends thought I was going crazy. They would bang on the door of my bedroom trying to get me to go out with them saying "Hey, let's go ingest more alcohol than our bodies can handle and then go bowling."[32] Because we all know that you bowl better that way. All I did was stay home and read my Bible. The reason I did this was because every time I opened that book, I learned something new.

Every time I read that book, I didn't want to stop. I was so hungry. Everything about Jesus spoke to my heart. People had always told me that "He died for your sins"- that he "sacrificed himself for you." But it never seemed real. I started reading his Word and for the first time in my life, Jesus seemed real.

There were things about Jesus that rocked my world. He hung out with dirty people (both literally and figuratively dirty). He ate dinner with people that were thieves. Good ole Zaccheaus was a wee little man that liked to pad his wallet with the hard earned money of others. Jesus looked at this little thief and said "Lets eat dinner at your house."

Jesus looked out over the open sea and yelled for a bunch of stinky fishermen to follow him. He hung out with them, he ate with them, and he laughed with them. He lived life with these stinky fishermen.

The bottom line is that he never turned away the hurting, the afflicted, and the disease-ridden. He went to them and helped them. When they came to him, he embraced them. That spoke to my heart because I was one of those afflicted and disease-ridden people. Jesus' humanity spoke to my heart because I so desperately wanted someone like that in my life. I wanted someone that wouldn't push me away. I wanted someone to accept me and all my faults. I wanted someone to love me despite my stupidity and failure. I wanted that. I needed that. Jesus was that and is that. After reading I knew I wasn't alone anymore. I knew I was going to be okay because I had Jesus in my life.

That's why he is 100% human. So that you could connect with him on a very personal level. So that you could look at him and say, "that's the kind of person I want to be." **His human nature connects with us on a personal level.**

Not Just a Man

Jesus doesn't stop there. If he does, then he's just another man- but he doesn't. He takes it to a whole new level. He never pushed away the contagious leper. He pulled them in close and did things that can't be done. He healed the lepers. With the words of Jesus, dead skin started to grow again. He didn't ignore the bleeding woman pulling on his robe. He freed her from her ailment. He did things like make a spit-mud pie and cake it in a blind guy's eyes. That spit-mud pie brought life to once broken eyes. He stood face to face with a raving madman possessed with demons and his words alone caused the demons to retreat, giving the man freedom and peace. He healed the sick. He cured disease. He fed enormous crowds of hungry people with food that would normally feed three or four people. Jesus did the impossible. **His divine nature connects with us on a much needed spiritual level.**

"Hole!"

One of my favorite stories is found in Luke 5. It's a story of friendship. It's a story of sin. It's a story of hatred. It's a story of redemption. This story literally has everything in it. The story starts in verse 17. Jesus was in a house teaching a bunch of pharisees. The pharisees were considered the spiritually elite of their day. They believed in obedience and following God's law. However, most pharisees were seen as hypocrites. Their relationship with God became more about rules and less about God. Jesus and the pharisees were in constant conflict because they sacrificed knowing God for a false sense of righteousness. Nevertheless, Jesus still spent time with them.

The crowd that was in this house was huge because the word had gotten out about Jesus and people were coming from everywhere just to get a glimpse of him. Some people were coming for another reason, including mere curiosity. They were sick or hurting and they desperately needed someone to heal them.

So Jesus was teaching this huge crowd and a group of men showed up carrying their paralyzed friend hoping that Jesus would heal him. The only problem was, they couldn't get to Jesus. This house was packed full of people and no one was going to get out of the way for a group of men to bring their crippled friend in. So they did the only thing they could think of, they climbed up on the roof and started ripping the ceiling apart.

Think about that for a second. Who does that? Who climbs onto someone else's roof and starts to destroy it? Can you imagine someone doing that to your house? It's ridiculous. Jesus was in the middle of teaching and people are hanging onto his every word. All of a sudden, the ceiling started to fall in and a grown man was slowly lowered down right in front of Jesus. If you're that man, what do you say as you're being lowered in front of Jesus? "What's up? Get it?" "Just thought I'd drop in." It's ridiculous, but that's what happened.

Jesus looked at the man, looked up at the now missing ceiling and he knew exactly what was going on. This is faith. Faith on the part of the friends for lowering the man down, but let's not forget about the faith of the man being lowered down as well. He looked back to the man in front of him and said the most important words this man ever heard in his entire life: **verse 20**: "When Jesus saw their faith, he said, 'Friend, your sins are forgiven.'"

Those were the most important words this man could have ever heard. Don't be mistaken- when he forgave this man, Jesus wasn't saying that the man was especially sinful or that his paralysis was directly caused by sin. No, he was addressing the man's greatest need; and the root of all pain and suffering- sin. And when Jesus did that he stepped beyond the boundaries of man. When man tries to forgive sin, this steps on God's toes. Only God can forgive sin and everyone who witnessed the exchange between the paralytic and Jesus knew it. **Verse 21**...

The Pharisees and the teachers of the law began thinking to themselves, "Who is this fellow who speaks blasphemy? Who can forgive sins but God alone?"

And guess what? They're right. Man can't forgive sins. Granted, you can forgive a person that has sinned against you, but the ultimate removal of sin can come only from God. They weren't wrong to think that a mere man can't and shouldn't be saying things like "your sins are forgiven." Only God solves the sin problem. So they were onto something... that is, unless they were mistaken about who Jesus actually was. Jesus, of course, knew everything the crowd was thinking in their hearts and he confronted them with the truth of who he was. The man was still lying on the mat, **verse 22**...

Jesus knew what they were thinking and asked, "Why are you thinking these things in your hearts? 23 Which is easier: to say, 'Your sins are forgiven,' or to say, 'Get up and walk'?

He gave them all a choice: "Would you rather me 'forgive' sins or tell him to 'walk?'" How about both? In **verse 23,** Jesus gave them the purpose of his miracles: But I want you to know that the Son of Man has authority on earth to forgive sins." So he said to the paralyzed man, "I tell you, get up, take your mat and go home." The miracle was always intended to provide a witness as to who Jesus was.

Hair In My Face

Have you ever had to prove who you are? How would you go about doing that? When I was a kid I always got bored shopping with my mom. My mother would always go up and down every single aisle looking for sales. Even if she didn't need it, if it was on sale she would get twenty of them. "Buy One Get One Free! I'll take ten of them!" She would come home with twelve bottles of conditioner. No shampoo just conditioner. Five bottles of the most obscure vitamin out there: "We need more B17 in our diet, we're not eating enough seeds!" A box of three hundred taquitos[33]. Can you even eat three hundred taquitos in a lifetime? They're not that good.

A shopping trip would last for a good three hours. Of course, I would wander off in search of my sanity in the toys section. After a while, I would realize that I was all alone and I would start to worry: "Where's my mom?"

An employee would walk me around the store to help me find my mom. When I did find her, I would run up to her yelling "Mommy, mommy!" Well my mom had a bit of a sick sense of humor. Every single time, she would pretend she didn't know me: "This isn't my son; I don't know who this child is!" This would go on for about ten minutes. Finally, my mom would say "Wait a minute." She would move the hair out of my eyes[34] and go "There you are... you are my son."

After about the one hundredth time, I finally started to just move my hair out of my eyes myself, "Are you kidding? It's me mom! You're the one that gave me this horrible haircut in the first place. I had no choice in the matter. You dressed me too; that's why I'm wearing a tie dye t-shirt with shorts that barely reach the tops of my thighs. I look like a jogging hippy![35] And why in the world are you buying thirty cans of cat food? We don't even have a cat!"

It was my mom's special way of identifying me and scarring me for life all at the same time. It's okay, I have decided that when she gets a little older I'm going to start doing the same thing to her. "I have no idea who this woman is; this isn't my mother!"[36]

Form of ID

How do you identify yourself? When a cop pulls you over and asks for your identification do you point to your face? When you go out of the country and they ask for your passport do you just say "It's me!" You can try but it won't work. No, you pull out your license or passport with the horrible looking picture[37] on it in order to prove who you are.

The miracle was always intended to provide a witness as to who Jesus was. When John the Baptist was in prison, he sent his followers to ask Jesus a question: "Are you the one who is to come, or should we expect someone else?"[38]

Jesus sends Johns followers back with this message, "Go back and report to John what you hear and see: The blind receive sight, the lame walk, those who have leprosy are cleansed, the deaf hear, the dead are raised, and the good news is proclaimed to the poor. Blessed is anyone who does not stumble on account of me."[39]

The miracles were always intended to confirm the divine power of Christ. They were a witness to say that "this is the Christ that you have all been waiting for." The miracles were his credentials. Therefore, what happens next in Luke 5 is vitally important. Jesus has forgiven the man's sins. He has boldly told the paralyzed man to stand up and go home.

What Happens Next

What the man does next is vitally important. If he just lies there, doesn't move, and doesn't walk then Jesus is just a man. If he does obey what Jesus has said, then Jesus is so much more.

"Immediately he stood up in front of them, took what he had been lying on and went home praising God. Everyone was amazed and gave praise to God. They were filled with awe and said, "We have seen remarkable things today."[40]

It's true, only God can forgive sins. What they failed to see was God right there in front of them in the form of Jesus. Which is easier: to forgive sins or to heal the sick? That is kind of a funny question. Jesus asked this question because he knew that for man this is impossible. But God is the full embodiment of the impossible and because of that, nothing is impossible for him. His authority and power are confirmed.

More Than A Carpenter

One of my favorite books of all time is Josh McDowell's *More Than A Carpenter*. If you have honest questions about Jesus, I encourage you to make this a staple in your library.[41] This book helped me to solidify my belief inGod. Chapter 3 is entitled "Liar, Lunatic, or Lord?" and it poses the question to us: Who do you believe he is? Is Jesus a liar (meaning that he isn't who he says he is)? Is he a lunatic (meaning that he was completely out of his mind)? Or, is He the Lord (meaning he was the perfect combination of two natures in one body)?

What did Jesus say about himself? He said, *"if you've seen me then you've seen the Father."*[42] He said, *"the*

father and I are one."[43] He said, *"I am the son of God."*[44]
McDowell writes...

> "Jesus claimed to be God, and to him it was of
> fundamental importance that men and women
> believed him to be who he was. Either we believe
> him, or we don't. He didn't leave us any wiggle
> room for in-between, watered-down alternatives.
> One who claimed what Jesus claimed about him-
> self couldn't be a good moral man or a prophet.
> That option isn't open to us, and Jesus never
> intended it to be."[45]

Jesus said it: "I am God." Now we have a decision to
make: true or false. Jesus didn't just let His words speak
for Him. He let the evidence speak for itself.

The fact that Jesus is fully man helps us to make
a very real emotional and human connection to him.
Understand that there is so much more to his humanity
that we will explore later in the next chapter. But at its
basis, his humanity helps us to connect with him.

But at the same time Jesus is also fully God and this
allows us to connect with him on a spiritual level. He did
the impossible in a body like ours. He defied our logic
while looking just like us. He wants us to believe the unbelievable. He wants it so much that he gave us all the evidence we would need. The miracles performed were: 1) to
confirm the message, 2) to confirm the messenger and 3)
most importantly, to produce faith. He does this because
God never sent his spokesman away empty handed. He
always gave them the proof, or evidence of divine power.
The signs that Jesus showed were unmistaken proof that

He was God. His divine power was shown so that we would believe the unbelievable. Sound impossible? Well, nothing is impossible with God.

What Do You Think?

1. Share something that is physically impossible for you to do.
2. In your own words, describe how Jesus is both fully God and fully man at the same time.
3. How does Jesus' humanity connect with you personally?
4. Why does John say in Luke 5:17, "And the power of the Lord was with Jesus to heal the sick?"
5. What point did Jesus want to draw from this incident when he said to the Pharisees '...which is easier to say? "Your sins are forgiven!" or "Get up, take your mat, and go home?"
6. Why did Jesus use the term "Son of Man" rather than "Son of God" or "Messiah?" See Daniel 7:13-14.
7. The miracles of our Lord force us to come to a decision concerning Jesus Christ. He was fully man and fully God. Author Josh McDowell writes that Jesus is either a liar, lunatic, or Lord. How do His miracles persuade you?

Chapter 4

"THE IMPOSSIBLE KNOT"

"Any concept of grace that makes us feel more comfortable sinning is not biblical grace. God's grace never encourages us to live in sin, on the contrary, it empowers us to say no to sin and yes to truth."
　　　　　　　　　　　　　　　　　—Randy Alcorn

Tales From the Fortune Cookie

A few years ago I did this sermon series called "Tales From the Fortune Cookie." My music minister Dana and I were eating a lot of Pei Wei's at the time. While waiting for our food, we would grab a handful of cookies, read the fortune, and of course make fun of how ridiculous they were. One day, Dana opened a cookie and read it. Honestly, it was a pretty good one. So I said, "that's a good one. I could probably even write a sermon based on that." That was all it took. All of the sudden, Dana and I are taking bags full of fortune cookies at a time from Pei Wei's and searching for sermon cookies. We got about five that worked. Dana made a trippy bumper video with a spinning panda head. We ordered four hundred custom-made fortune cookies with these fortunes in them. Every sermon was started by opening the fortune cookie.

Worst Fortune Cookie Fortunes

You have to be real careful with a sermon series like this, because there are some pretty horrible fortunes out there. I was doing a lot of research on the topic and here is a list of the worst fortune cookie fortunes I could find that people actually received.

1. "What? Three servings of Moo Shoo Pork weren't enough for you tubby?"
2. "Your fullness will be short-lived... like an hour, tops."
3. "Put all your money and jewelry in the egg roll and nobody gets hurt."
4. "Creative Chinese chef without utensils can still find ways to stir soup."
5. "Man who look to stale cookie for advice probably make good busboy. Ask waitress for application."
6. "Your strength lies in your continued belief that what you just ate was indeed duck."
7. "Patron who mocks waiter's accent will unwittingly consume chef's bodily fluids."
8. "Today's dog in alley is tomorrow's moo goo gai pan."

What would you do if your minister opened up a fortune cookie for a sermon topic and it said "Today's dog in the alley is tomorrow's moo goo gai pan." You know they would try to spin it to make some kind sense, "and then

God told Peter to get up kill and eat, so I guess eating dog is all right." Throughout the entire series I was extremely paranoid that I would open the wrong fortune when we opened up the cookies. That would teach me to mock the waiter. It never did happen and it turned out to be a great sermon series. One fortune, however, stuck out to me more than all the others.

To Think is Easy, To Act is Difficult.
To Act As One Thinks is the Most Difficult of All.[46]

Yeah, I know... you're doing the same thing that Dana and I did when we first read it: Staring blankly and reading it again slowly. It's kind of a confusing, a bit hard to understand, but then again I think that's how the Christian life is at times. Because of sin, the Christian life can be very confusing.

The Legend of the Gordian Knot

Actually, sometimes I feel like it can be likened to a knot. And not just any kind of knot. Have you ever heard the legend of the Gordian Knot? The actual definition of the Gordian Knot is this... An exceedingly complicated problem or deadlock. To be a bit more literal, it's an unsolvable knot.

According to an ancient Greek legend, a poor peasant called Gordius arrived with his wife in the public square of Phrygia in an ox cart. As chance would have it, an oracle had previously informed the people that their future king would come into town riding in a wagon. Seeing Gordius, the people made him king. In gratitude, Gordius dedicated his ox cart to Zeus, tying it up with a highly intricate knot—the Gordian knot. Another oracle foretold that the person who untied the knot would rule all of Asia.

But Gordian's Knot resisted all attempts to solve it until the year 333 B.C. when Alexander the Great stepped onto the scene. Not known for his lack of ambition when it came to ruling Asia, he looked at the knot, contemplated the puzzle before him, then he took his sword out and cut through it. He finally solved the puzzle of the Gordian Knot.

The Justin Knot

I don't have a Gordian Knot. What I have is what I like to call the **Justin Knot**. It's horrendous. My knot is seemingly impossible to untie. You all have your own knots as well. What I want you to do is to name your own knot after yourself: **The _____ Knot**. We all have our own knots and these knots represent our seemingly impossible struggle with sin. Write that down next to your knot, "**= seemingly impossible struggle with sin**."

Our struggle with sin is like a Gordian knot: it seems like there's no end. And of course the more we struggle with trying to untie the knot, the worse it gets until we are frustrated and exasperated to the point of almost giving up. What we need is a sword, just like Alexander to cut through the knot. The good news is that we have that sword. His name is Jesus. He cuts through our sin problem as a result of his humanity.

Poop-Eating Dog

Are you perfect? If you'd like, you can go ahead and raise your hand to identify your perfection. Don't worry, the people around you won't know why you're raising your hand. If they did, they would call you a liar to your face. Why? Because it's impossible. The human nature is sinful. We are attracted to sin. We are drawn to sin. We are drawn to sin like a homemade meal. Scripture however describes it differently. Scripture says "As a dog returns to its vomit, so a fool repeats his folly."[47] Have you ever seen your dog do this? They eat it like it's filet mignon, but the look on their face says "this is disgusting." I used to have a dog that didn't just eat her own vomit. I had a dog that would go to the bathroom and then immediately turn around and start eating it. For the longest time I couldn't figure out why her breath smelled so bad. Then one day I caught her in the act and I said, "what in the world are you doing?" The look on her face said, "I don't know!!!"

Don't Do It!

We all know how that feels. When you were a kid, you could get away with it. Your mom or dad would tell you not to do something and of course what did you do? That which they told you not to do. I remember my parents said all the time "Why do you always do what I tell you not to?" I always thought to myself, "I'm going to tell my son what to do and he's going to do it. That's the bottom line." Then one day it happened.

Jonas was touching my TV and I said, "Jonas, don't touch the TV, you're going to get your finger prints all over it." I'm a good parent so I always give my son an explanation as to "why." He stopped but a minute later he was right back at it. "Jonas, stop touching the TV." He stopped again, but of course in no time he was right back at it. So I said, "Jonas this is your last warning, stop touching the TV." I'm also a merciful parent, so I give my son four strikes before he's out. This time I watched him the whole time and guess what? He was watching me too. He just couldn't help himself, as he was staring me down, that hand slowly rose up to touch the TV. "Don't you do it Jonas!" He paused, then the hand moved again. "Don't!" He stopped again, then all of a sudden, he touched. I jumped up yelling "THAT'S IT BABY, YOUR BUTT IS MINE NOW!!!"[48]

It's amazing. He knew he was not supposed to do it. He knew that it made me unhappy. He knew it was wrong because I could see it in his eyes. He just couldn't help himself. Kind of like you and me. It looks like our struggle with sin, doesn't it? Kind of looks like our knot. Unfortunately, we don't have the excuse "I'm a cute little baby and can get away with it."

Paul's Knot

We are just like that when it comes to sin. We know it's wrong and we don't want to do it, but... we keep doing it. I know that a lot of you are reading this thinking to yourself, "yep that just described me." If I just described you, I don't want you to feel bad, because you're in some pretty good company. **Romans 7:14-20** is what I like to call **Paul's Knot**. listen to this:

> "We know that the law is spiritual; but I am unspiritual, sold as a slave to sin. I do not understand what I do. For what I want to do I do not do, but what I hate I do. And if I do what I do not want to do, I agree that the law is good. As it is, it is no longer I myself who do it, but it is sin living

in me. I know that nothing good lives in me, that
is, in my sinful nature. For I have the desire to do
what is good, but I cannot carry it out. For what
I do is not the good I want to do; no, the evil I do
not want to do — this I keep on doing."[49]

This passage of Scripture describes Paul's constant
and ongoing struggle with sin. He has his very own knot
just like you and me. Paul faced the same daily battle in
his mind, heart, and emotions that you and I face and God
used him to write two-thirds of the new testament! You're
in good company.

Now of course when you read something like this your
mind automatically starts running,... "Oh my gosh what
did he do? It sounds so bad and naughty." The truth is that
we don't know exactly what his struggle was. We see Paul
refer to a **"thorn in his flesh."**[50]

Countless explanations have been offered concerning
the nature of Paul's thorn in the flesh. Everything from
speech disability, to physical problems (such as eye problems, malaria, migraine headaches, and epilepsy), all the
way to sexual issues. We know that in Paul's day sexual
sin was extremely common. In that same verse, Paul talks
about coveting, but he applies it to others rather than himself: he isn't saying "hey, this is what I do." There is no
way know exactly what Paul's thorn in the flesh is, but
what we do know is that this indwelling sin had a certain
power over him. This sin secured a powerful foothold on
him and made Paul's body its home.

Paul used words like **"law"** and **"slavery"** which paint
a very graphic picture of what a powerful hold this deep-
seated sin had over Paul. It was if they were his master.

Paul felt forced to carry out what he did not want to do, what he really hated, whereas what he would like to have done never seemed to happen. Paul had a sin knot just like every single one of us has.

Paul's struggle with sin reflects our own. Our sin is a mess that we want out of our lives, but honestly, at times feel powerless to overcome it. When Paul was at his lowest, what did he say "What a wretched man I am! Who will rescue me from this body of death? (or this struggle with sin) Thanks be to God — through Jesus Christ our Lord!"[51]

His Perfection

How many of you can claim that you are sinless? Let's ask it this way: how many humans in all of history can claim to have lived a sinless life? Only one. In the beginning, he was with God and he was God. He was born of a virgin by the work of the Holy Spirit. His name is Jesus.

Isaiah prophesied about his sinlessness when he said, "though he had done no violence, nor was any deceit in his mouth."[52] Peter reiterated this when he wrote "He committed no sin, and no deceit was found in his mouth."[53] There was no sin that was connected to the person of Jesus. The author of Hebrews described it best when he said "Such a high priest meets our need—one who is holy, blameless, pure, set apart from sinners, exalted above the heavens."[54]

The Blueprint of Temptation

I was thinking about how sin infects our life through temptation. Temptation has a very specific blueprint. It kind of goes like this:

1) Whatever you struggle with the most, that's what you will be tempted with the most. If your biggest struggle is a drug addiction, you're not going to be tempted with lust.
2) You will be tempted at the absolute worst time. It will happen at your weakest moment. When you're tired, hungry or depressed.
3) It's going to look like the best thing in the world at the time. Deep down inside, you will know that it's wrong and bad for you, but for some reason, that will not be at the forefront of your mind.
4) You will say no at first, but it's not a solid no. You will come up with some lame excuse like, "I'd love to, but I really have to go and groom my cat" instead of saying "No, that's sin and I can't do it." You'll say "I have to go home and watch re-runs of the office" instead of saying "I won't allow sin in my life."
5) You will fall.

That's the basic blueprint of temptation that leads us to a life of sin. We all seem to fall in line with this blueprint. You expose yourself to temptation and the next thing you know sin has become a full blown life threatening disease.

Jesus was 100% God. At the same time, he was 100% man as well. It was in his humanity that overcame sin.

The Temptation

In **Matthew 4,** we see the Jesus defy the blueprint of temptation. Jesus was tempted in all the ways we are tempted. Satan tempted Jesus at the most inopportune time: "After fasting forty days and forty nights, he was hungry. The tempter came to him...". [55] He was weak and hungry and that is exactly when Satan attacked, just like he would you or I.

He tempted Jesus to use his divine power to turn rocks into loaves of bread so that he could have something to eat. Jesus said "No!" It wasn't a fragile "no" like ours, it's a rock-hard "NO!" He quoted scripture: 'Man shall not live on bread alone, but on every word that comes from the mouth of God.'[56]

Satan tempted Jesus to throw himself off the top of a temple with the hook, "God will save you." This time, Satan even used scripture in order to convince Jesus.[57] Jesus responds with another powerful "NO!" and countered Satan's attacks with more scripture: "It is also written: 'Do not put the Lord your God to the test.'"[58]

Finally, Satan tempted him with power and authority, offering to give Jesus rule over the entire world if Jesus would just bow down and worship Him. Every time Satan attacks Jesus, he fights back. Jesus takes the battle to Satan: "Away from me, Satan! For it is written: "worship the Lord your God, and serve him only.'"[59] With that final stand, Jesus accomplished all that we fail to do. He succeeded in overcoming the temptation every single one of us falls to.

Sacrifices

This is why the humanity of Jesus is so important to us. Yes, His humanity helps us to connect with Him on a very personal level, but there is so much more to it than just that. The author of Hebrews writes "without the shedding of blood there is no forgiveness."[60] Animal sacrifice is a very important theme that we see throughout the Old Testament. Both Cain and Abel brought sacrifices to God. Cain's offering wasn't acceptable because it was fruit.[61] Able's sacrifice was accepted because it was the "first-born of his flock."[62] The first thing Noah did when the flood waters receded was to make an animal sacrifice.[63]

God required animal sacrifices in order to provide a temporary sin atonement.[64] God gave certain parameters to the sacrifices as well. 1) The animal being sacrificed had to be spotless. It had to be the best- not the weakest and lame- but the best. 2) The person doing the sacrificing had to identify with the animal. 3) The person offering the sacrifice had to kill the animal. When this was done, it offered a temporary forgiveness of sin.

The problem is that an animal sacrifice can only provide temporary forgiveness. While the sacrifice was supposed to be the best of the flock, it could never be a perfect sacrifice. That's where Jesus comes in. John the Baptist recognized this when he saw Jesus coming to be baptized and said, "Look, the lamb of God who takes away the sin of the world!"[65]

We needed Jesus to be a man that lived a completely sinless life so that our sins could be removed. He gave himself as a sacrifice for the sins of the whole world for all time. Jesus Christ took our sin upon Himself and died in our place. As Paul says, "God made him [Jesus] who had no sin to be sin for us, so that in him we might become the righteousness of God."[66] Through faith in what Jesus Christ accomplished on the cross, we can receive forgiveness. Jesus is the sword that cuts the sin knot that all of us struggle with.

Stop It!

Our struggle is seemingly impossible not because it actually is impossible but that we make it impossible. God doesn't make it impossible, **"for nothing is impossible with God."** The answer to our struggle is not untying the knot- it's in cutting the knot.

One time, a woman went to a therapist and she told him "I'm afraid of germs." He looked at her and said, "And?" She said, "Well, I'm so afraid of germs that I wash my hands over and over and over again until they start bleeding." He looked up from his notes and said "And?" She continued, "I'm so afraid of germs that sometimes I don't even leave the house because I'm afraid of touching the doorknob." This time he didn't even look up, he just said "And?" The lady at this point got really angry "'And?' What do you mean 'And?' My life is ruined! Tell me what to do!" The counselor asked, "Do you want me to tell you what to do?" "Yes, please, my life is a mess and I need help. What should I do?" Then he looked her in the eyes and calmly said "Stop It." "What? What do you mean stop it!" Then he yelled at her "Just stop it!" She started to panic because he started yelling louder and louder, "Stop it! Stop it! Stop it!"

Okay, that's horrible counseling, but it's great advice when it comes to our struggle with sin. And it's actually Paul's advice to dealing with sin. God inspired Paul to write these down these words: "Come back to your senses as you ought, and stop sinning; for there are some who are ignorant of God — I say this to your shame."[67]

This isn't a difficult verse to understand at all. I don't have to break out the Greek to bring out the meaning of this verse. He's saying, **"stop it! Stop sinning!"** Notice what Paul said just before he said "stop it."

The NIV says, **"come back to your senses."** The King James Version says it a little differently, **"awake to righteousness and sin not."** Another translation says, **"be awake to righteousness and keep yourselves from sin."** Another translation says, **"come to your right mind, and sin no more."**

Right Mind?

What is ones's "right mind"? What is "coming back to your senses", as the NIV says? Paul says in **1 Corinthians 2** that "we have the mind of Christ" and it basically means that we have the mind that understands the spiritual. Come back to the mindset that you have been made righteous through Christ. Awake to that knowledge and stop sinning. You can only stop it when you realize that you have been set free by the sacrifice of God. **Awake and Stop It!**

Awake to righteousness and sin not. Most of the time we think of that backwards- that I must stop sinning first before I can awake to righteousness. You have no idea how many people think this way. I've been told countless times, "I'll come back to church when I have everything under control." Or basically, when I get my knot untied, then I'll be back.

But that's not what it says. The Bible says first to awaken to righteousness. Then when we realize that we already are the righteousness of God- because he has made us his righteousness- then through that knowledge, and through the power and authority of his righteousness we will be able to overcome sin. Sin will no longer have any dominion over us. **Awake and stop it!**

Cut The Knot

Back a few years ago I had this revelation when it came to our struggle with sin and the whole idea with "Stop It!" I had a lot of fun preaching it. My students liked it a lot, they came up to me afterwards saying, "that was awesome. That was great advice." Some actually came up and said, "We should make a t-shirt out of that." Yeah, that's cool. My sermon inspires t-shirts. Why stop there? Lets go with key chains and coffee mugs. You know what? WWJD, get out of the way, here comes "Stop It!" Kids will be walking around with "Stop It" paraphernalia. That would have been awesome right?

Looking back years later I thought to myself, you know what would be cooler? If people would actually take the advice instead of figuring a way to market it. Forget the t-shirts, **just awake and stop it**. No coffee mugs, **just awake and stop it**. WWJD, you can have the market cornered on crappy bracelets**, just awake and stop it**. What would it mean for God's church if we came to our senses and stopped sinning?

Many, many, many years had past and the Gordian Knot could not be figured out. Men would come and fail to untie the knot, maybe even making it worse. And it went on for years. It was seemingly impossible to figure out. The truth was that it was actually pretty easy to figure out. Just cut the knot.

To Think is Easy, To Act is Difficult.
To Act As One Thinks is the Most Difficult of All.

Yes, it is. However, when we awake to the knowledge that we have been set free from the struggle of sin through the impossible God, then actually the answer is a lot easier than we think. Sometimes, we just need to cut the knot.

What do you think?

1. Read Romans 7:14-20? What are the characteristics of a slave?
2. What does this passage show about the nature of sin?
3. Describe examples of people living "as [slaves] to sin."
4. What are some examples of "what I want to do I do not do, but what I hate I do?" What is my hope against this sinful self?
5. In Matthew 4:1-11 we find the temptation of Jesus. Why do you think Jesus went into the wilderness for 40 days?
6. How does Jesus respond to each temptation? What does this teach us about our response to temptation?
7. Paul tells us that we must "come to our senses and stop sinning." How does Jesus make this possible in your life?

Chapter 5

"GOD: COSMIC KILLJOY?"

"Laughter is the most beautiful and beneficial therapy
God ever granted humanity."   –Chuck Swindoll

D oes God have a sense of humor? This is where the old pastor joke fits: "If you need proof that God has a sense of humor, just look in the mirror." That joke isn't too far off. There are many misconceptions about God. One that I find the most bizarre is that God is opposed to laughter and fun. God is seen as the fun police. The second you begin to enjoy yourself, God is right there to shut it down. "There will be no 'joking around'! There will be no laughter! There will be no playing! There will be no fun! You will not enjoy any part of life! Not while I'm on duty!"

This couldn't be further from the truth. God does not exist to spoil your fun. God is not the "Fun Police." God is not a "Cosmic Killjoy." Actually, the truth is quite the opposite. God does have a sense of humor. How do I know that? Because you have a sense of humor. And you are created in his image.

His Immutable Quality

Go ahead and look in the mirror. Maybe your hair is standing up in the back and not on purpose. Maybe your nose is bigger than the average nose. Maybe your ears can be compared to a famous Disney elephant. Maybe one of your eyes looks straight ahead while the other one is all over the place.[68] Maybe you are a young man that is trying to grow a beard, but all you can grow is a bea-. Maybe you're a young woman that has more facial hair than most young men–I'm sorry. Just look at yourself in the mirror. Now read this verse to yourself:

"So God created mankind in his own image, in the image of God he created them; male and female he created them."[69]

Now go ahead and feel free to laugh as loud as you want. You were made to laugh. The American Heritage Dictionary defines a "sense of humor" as "...The ability to perceive, enjoy, or express what is comical or funny." If we are created in his image, then God must show an ability to perceive what is comical. You were made to laugh. How can his creation think things are funny unless the whole idea came from God in the first place?

I believe that laugher is one of God's immutable qualities. We don't talk about this quality as much as others. God is love. God is power. God is holy. God is sovereign. God is merciful. God is righteous. God is funny? We don't talk about that too much. For the longest time God has been portrayed like the grumpy old man that doesn't want kids on his lawn. When the truth is, God is funny.

He's more like the practical jokester that makes everyone laugh than the guy that wants to complain about taxes being too high. Why not talk about his sense of humor?

You don't have to look far in God's word to see his humor. Alfred North Whitehead claimed *"the total absence of humor from the Bible is one of the most singular things in all of literature."* He felt like the circumstances of the Israelites in the Old Testament, continually attacked and overrun by foreign nations, "depressed" the people of God. So he failed to see any kind of humor in God's word. Well, he was wrong.

Elijah the Baal Buster

In the great showdown at Mount Carmel between Elijah and the prophets of Baal, it was one against four hundred and fifty. Elijah was the lone prophet of God standing before an army of Baal prophets. In order to prove whose god was the one true God, two alters were set up and the line was drawn:

Then Elijah said to them, "I am the only one of the Lord's prophets left, but Baal has four hundred and fifty prophets. Get two bulls for us. Let Baal's prophets choose one for themselves, and let them cut it into pieces and put it on the wood but not set fire to it. I will prepare the other bull and put it on the wood but not set fire to it. Then you call on the name of your god, and I will call on the name of the Lord. The god who answers by fire—he is God." Then all the people said, "What you say is good." Elijah said to the prophets of Baal, "Choose one of the bulls and prepare it first, since there are so many of you. Call on the name of your god, but do not light the fire." So they took the bull given them and prepared it.[70]

The prophets of Baal prayed for fire. They shouted at the top of their lungs. They danced around the alter in hopes that Baal would answer them. The entire time Elijah sat back and mocked them:

27 At noon Elijah began to taunt them. "Shout louder!" he said. "Surely he is a god! Perhaps he is deep in thought, or busy, or traveling. Maybe he is sleeping and must be awakened."[71]

Some say that Elijah's irony bordered on sarcasm. There is no "bordering" here. It's sarcasm at it best. The mocking tone in Elijah's words are easily heard, but what exactly is he saying when he suggest that Baal is "busy"? What could Baal be so "busy" doing that he can't answer the prayers of his followers? Some might not like this but the Hebrew language says: "Maybe he is going to the bathroom..." or as the New Living Translation puts it "he may be relieving himself...". That's funny.

I Don't Remember Eating That!

Take the story of Jonah. Here you have a grown man acting like a child. God gives him a job to do. Jonah was charged with going to Ninevah and preaching against their growing wickedness. Instead, Jonah ran to Tarshish. That was 2,500 miles east of Israel in the opposite direction of Ninevah. To say that Jonah hated the Ninevites is an understatement. Jonah hated them so much that he did everything humanly possible to try and avoid God saving the Ninevites. When he got to Tarshish, he boarded a ship. Something you need to know about God: you can't stop God from showing mercy. You can't stop God from doing anything.

God sent a storm that threatened the entire ship. Everyone was so afraid that they started to throw their cargo overboard in hopes of surviving. When the crew found out that Jonah was the problem, they threw him overboard too.

"Now the Lord provided a huge fish to swallow Jonah, and Jonah was in the belly of the fish three days and three nights."[72]

God uses this giant fish to transport his prophet back on track to Ninevah. After those three days and three nights in the belly of the giant fish God commanded the fish and he "vomited Jonah on dry land."[73]

We've all been sick before. Things coming back up never look the same as when they went down. It's believed that Jonah's skin was bleached white from the digestive juices of the fishes stomach. Not only did Jonah still have to preach to the Ninevites, he had to do it looking like a ghost that spent too much time in the bath tub and of course smelled a bit fishy.

Have you ever gotten sick and thought to yourself "I don't remember eating that." Now think about what was going through the fish's mind that just vomited a grown man that was still alive. "I don't remember eating this guy." That's funny.

Be Still, I'm Going Back to Bed.

One day Jesus and his disciples decided to go on a cruise. That, of course, is my translation. They left a large crowd behind and decided to get away. While on the board a huge storm started to pick up and the disciples started to panic. The waves were crashing into the small boat. As the boat started to take on water, I picture that the disciples were frantically doing everything they could so that they boat wouldn't sink. Where was Jesus? "Jesus was in the stern, sleeping on a cushion."[74]

So the boat was sinking and Jesus was taking a nap. Finally, the disciples decided to wake Jesus up. "Teacher, don't you care if we drown?"[75] Scripture says that Jesus woke up and told the storm to stop it—and it did. The picture I have in my head every time I read this story goes like this: Jesus walks onto the deck rubbing the sleep from his eyes. He sees the raging waves all around them. He raises a hand and says "Be still." The waves obey. Jesus then says "I'm going back to bed." That's funny.

"Secret Parts"

I have a friend that likes to tell the story in 1 Samuel 5 when the Philistines stole the ark of the Lord and all the troubles that it caused them. This is one of those lesson we all need to learn: Don't mess with God.

The Philistines put the ark of the Lord before their god Dagon. The next morning the Philistines found the statue of Dagon face first on the ground before the ark of God. Don't mess with God. They picked Dagon up and put him back in his place standing before the ark. The next day, Dagon fell again. This time his head and hands had fallen off as well. The statue was little more than a stump bowing before the ark of God. Don't mess with God.

Then God decided to stop messing around with the Philistines and he got nasty with them. "He afflicted the people of the city, both young and old, with an outbreak of tumors."[76] That word "tumor" also translates from the Hebrew as "hemorrhoid." The King James Version gives us the clearest picture when it says that God gave them hemorrhoids on their "secret parts." Don't mess with God. He may just give you hemorrhoids on your "secret parts." That's funny. Painful sounding, but still funny.

To The Fullest

God's word is full of stories just like these that show the immutable quality of God's sense of humor. God is funny. God wants you to laugh. That leads me to the conclusion that God wants you to enjoy life. Let me explain further.

In **John 10** we have a contrast between the good shepherd and the false prophets of Israel. Jesus is the true, legitimate shepherd who wants us to enjoy life. Jesus told us, "The thief comes only to steal and kill and destroy; I have come that they may have life, and have it to the full."[77] Life "to the full" doesn't sound like a gift from someone that is against joy and pleasure. Jesus didn't come here so that you could be bored to death. Jesus didn't come so that you could be disinterested in life. Jesus didn't come so that you would be sick and tired of life— "When's it going to be over?" Jesus came so that you could experience the full myriad of joy and pleasure of this life. But for some reason, most people on the outside looking in don't see Christians living this way. They don't see Christians enjoying life. They don't see Christians laughing. They don't see Christians having any fun. On the rare chance that a Christian is having fun they are quickly labeled a hypocrite or sinner by those outside the church as well as those inside the church. Why is that?

Synonym of Sin?

For the longest time the church has treated fun as a synonym of sin. We've treated sin and laughter as the same thing. It's true that some sin is fun. There are some Christians that will tell you that sin isn't fun. Not only are they wrong, they're liars too. If sin wasn't fun then we wouldn't have a problem with it. If sin wasn't associated with a good time then preachers would be out of a job. You can't deny it. There is a connection between sin and fun. But it's not what you think.

Eczema is a condition that causes the skin to become itchy and inflamed. My oldest son has eczema. Sometimes it's so bad that it has woken him up in the middle of the night. It drives him nuts, he starts to scratch and can't stop. Next thing you know his legs and arms are all scratched up and sometimes they're bleeding. He has a prescription oil that we have to put on his entire body at least once a week.

Sin is a lot like Eczema. When you itch the infected area, it feels great. However, the more you scratch it the redder it gets. Yet you still find pleasure in itching it, so you keep doing it. Next thing you know you're drawing blood. But it still feels good so you keep itching. Eventually it stops itching, but now it hurts and burns. You would have been better not itching it at all and using an ointment or lotion. Now it's too late. You enjoyed the pleasure of scratching for too long.

You can't argue that the body enjoys sin. **Galatians 5** shows us how our flesh is made to enjoy sin. In **Hebrews 11** Moses chose God and his people over the "pleasures of sin."[78] There is a form of pleasure found in sin. However, the pleasure that sin produces is not a lasting pleasure. It's just for a time. It's just for a season. The author of Hebrews says that pleasure is "fleeting." You enjoy it for a time, and then it's gone.

Creator of Pleasure

It's true that sin is fun, but not all fun is sin. The mistake Christians have made in the past is to connect all fun with sin. Not only does that sound ridiculous, it's Biblically untrue. God want's you to experience life to it's fullest. God wants you to laugh. God wants you to have fun because God is the creator of pleasure.

Looking at the life of Jesus we can see that he was anything but a killjoy. The first miracle Jesus performed was at a wedding. The celebration was in full swing when the unthinkable happened: they ran out of wine. What did Jesus do? Did he say "Good, drinking wine is a sin."? No, he turned regular old water into the best wine they had ever had.

Have you ever seen little kids around a boring and grumpy adult? They don't want anything to do with him. If Jesus is a killjoy, the children would have wanted nothing to do with him. But that's not what we see in scripture. The children flocked to Jesus and he loved being with them. Jesus enjoyed life because there is a connection between a "full life" and pleasure.

God created you to experience pleasure. You can enjoy a slice of pizza because of those taste buds that he created. The next time you get a Midnight Chocolate Truffle Blizzard from Dairy Queen, take one bite and praise God.

God created your eyes to experience joy at the sight of color. When the fireworks soar into the air and explode into different colors and shapes and all you can say in response is "wow," Praise God. He created your eyes to enjoy that experience.

I don't mean to be crude here, but God did create both man and woman to be perfectly compatible. God gave the married couple the ability to show their love to each other in a very special way. Sex[79] was God's idea. How in the world can you ever think that God is a cosmic killjoy? He created sex!

Fully Know Him

It's the one topic that we hardly ever talk about, yet you can't deny it. You are created in his image. You were created to laugh. My staff meetings at church are filled with laughter. I work with some of the funniest people in the world. My church services are filled with laughter. A church that laughs together, grows together. My home is filled with laughter. Between myself, my wonderful wife, my two sons, and an aging chihuahua, the laughter is endless. And that's a great thing because that's how God created us.

His sense of humor is one of God's most underrated characteristics. But open up his word and you don't have to look far to find funny. Did you know that two random bears maul 42 youth because they were teasing Elisha about being bald? Or that Paul preached too long and a guy fell asleep, fell out a window and died. Did you know that there's a talking ass (donkey) in scripture? You don't have to go too far to find funny.

And God wanted you to enjoy the time you have. Not by sinning, but by fully understanding who he is. Jesus came to this earth so that you would have an abundant life. That sounds enjoyable. When you laugh it's because you were created to laugh. You were designed to have fun. You were made to enjoy life. Until you understand fun and laughter as one of God's immutable characteristics, not only can you not fully appreciate him, but you can't fully know him.

What do you think?

1. What are some other funny stories in scripture that have caught your attention? (I'm sure I missed a few)
2. Prior to reading this chapter, did you have a view of God as a "Cosmic Killjoy?" What caused you to view God this way?
3. How does it make you feel to see that God has a sense of humor?
4. God wants you to have a full life. How can understanding this characteristic about him help you in living a full life?

Chapter 6

"EXCLUSIVE?"

> "We must never allow the authority of books, institutions, or leaders to replace the authority of 'knowing' Jesus Christ personally and directly. When the religious views of others interpose between us and the primary experience of Jesus as the Christ, we become unconvicted and unpersuasive travel agents handing out brochures to places we have never visited."   – Brenning Manning

Has anyone ever looked at you and given you this excuse: "I'm only human." As opposed to what? What's the other option? What is everyone else's excuse? This is one of those things that we say that just doesn't make sense.

Or how about when someone is trying to explain something they've seen and they say, "I saw it with my own eyes." Really? As opposed to someone else's eyes? Now I'm convinced. Although I would be more impressed if you had accomplished that with someone else's eyes.

I say this one all the time, and it makes me mad but it just pops out of my mouth. What about when someone says "Same difference." I admit that I say that one. Basically, the people like me that use this phrase are saying that we either don't know what the word "same" means or we don't know what the word "difference" means, or both. I realize that when I say it, I am saying "I don't care."

Or when someone is trying to explain how simple something is, they say "It's a piece of cake." First of all, have you ever heard someone say "it's a piece of cake" when referring to an actual piece of cake? And when did cake become synonymous with simplicity? Have you ever tried to make a cake from scratch without any instructions? I can't do it. And if you can do it, it's still not easy enough to be considered the poster child for ease. Pancake- now those are simple. "Easy as a pancake!" I know it sounds stupid, but it's more fitting than cake. Here's another alternative: "Easy as ordering pizza!" You can do that online now, it's so easy.

What about when someone looks at you and says "Two heads are better than one." Not necessarily. When you add another head into the equation you have now made it possible to "bump heads." In addition, it really does depend on the heads in question. If you have two whose combined IQ is still below a 60, you're not doing any better. One head is looking at the problem going, "that's a piece of cake!" The other head's going "ehhhh, same difference." Two heads aren't always better than one. When my younger brother and I got together, we would blow stuff up. We didn't set out to blow stuff up, it just happened on account of the two heads deal. These are some weird things we say. They're kind of ridiculous when you think about it. They're actually a bit outrageous.

Jesus said some pretty outrageous things. Some of the things Jesus said were flat out hard to swallow and were probably really offensive to certain people. People would walk away saying "I can't believe he said that" or "He said what?" Chances are, you've sat down to read Scripture and gotten to one of these and it has completely confused you. For example, in Revelation 3, Jesus said that because you're these lukewarm followers "you make me want to vomit you out of my mouth." That's kind of mean to say. Isn't Jesus supposed to be the nice guy? Or what do you think people's reaction was in Matthew 25 when he said "I was naked and you didn't clothe me." That had to make everyone a little uncomfortable. "When did we see Jesus naked?" Or how about when he stood up before everyone in Matthew 18 and told everyone to gouge their eyes out. It's a bit extreme and people walked about thinking just that. Jesus said some pretty outrageous- even impossible things- about himself.

The verse that jumps out to me is a verse that has to do with the exclusivity of the Gospel. I've noticed the problem this way: people love Jesus. Even if you don't love him, you think he's a pretty cool guy and you respect him. But at the same time, you don't like being told what to do. You're the kind of person that goes on a road trip, gets lost, and refuses to ask for directions. Even if you did ask for directions, you would walk away going "there has to be an easier way!" The verse I am referring to is **John 14:6** where Jesus said ... "I am the way and the truth and the life. No one comes to the Father except through me."

Mutually Exclusive Events

Have you ever heard of mutually exclusive events? Basically, two events are mutually exclusive if they cannot occur at the same time. This is pretty cool. For example, you cannot turn your head both left and right at the same time. You can turn your head left and scratch your head at the same time. That's not mutually exclusive. Or in cards, you can have a King of Hearts or an Ace of Hearts, but you cannot have an Ace of Kings. They're mutually exclusive.

The best example is the coin toss. We use it in sporting events. We use coin tosses in football to determine who is going to be on offense first. We use it here at our church also to decide on who is going to get the last doughnut between two of my staff members. Fay and I used this to name our kids. Heads we call him Tobias Larkin. Tails, it's Chalupa Batman[80] Larkin... Tobias it is. The coin toss is a mutually exclusive event.

When you toss a coin, it cannot land on both heads and tails. Logically, it cannot happen. It's either one or the other. For those of you who refuse to accept this and say something along the lines of "What if the coin lands on it's side? Wouldn't that be both heads and tails at the same time?" The answer to that is a two fold answer. First of all, the probability of that actually happening is highly unlikely. They did the probability of a nickel landing on the edge and found out that it's 1 in 6,000. The second answer is "NO!" It's the edge, not the heads or the tails. You want to know who wins that, the person flipping the coin. That means I get the last doughnut. A mutually exclusive event is two events that cannot occur at the same time.

Jesus, The Mutually Exclusive Event

Now, according to scripture, the gospel is a mutually exclusive event. This means that you cannot be with God by going through anyone else other than Jesus. Turn to John 14. The chapter before 14 is actually where everything starts to unfold. And it's a pretty somber moment. This was the last time Jesus will be with everyone before the crucifixion. The disciples had no clue what was about to happen or even what was happening at the moment. Jesus knew everything so he started to talk to them about what was about to happen. He was starting to prepare their hearts. He started off by washing their feet to show them how he came to serve them and the whole world. He told them about how he was going to be betrayed and how he was going to be leaving them soon. So naturally, the disciples were a little down. In chapter 14, verses 1-4, Jesus is trying to encourage them...

"Do not let your hearts be troubled. You believe in God; believe also in me. My Father's house has many rooms; if that were not so, would I have told you that I am going there to prepare a place for you? And if I go and prepare a place for you, I will come back and take you to be with me that you also may be where I am. You know the way to the place where I am going."

Remember when I told you that the disciples were clueless about what was going on. This was the standard when it came to the disciples. They were pretty much always clueless and when Jesus said this, the group's clueless spokesman spoke up. Thomas, said to him, "Lord, we don't know where you are going, so how can we know the way?"[81] Translation: "Ummm, we have no clue what's going on." That right there was what triggered

Jesus to say "I am the way and the truth and the life. No one comes to the Father except through me."[82]

That's what Jesus said about himself and in light of certain events it was kind of conflicting. Jesus' way would be the cross. He would be convicted by blatant liars. His body would soon lie lifeless in a tomb. Because he accepted that way, he is the way to God. Because he did not contest the lies, we can believe He is the truth. Because he was willing to die, he becomes the channel of resurrection—our life.

Is Jesus the Only Way?

The hardest part, however, is that last sentence. Most people have no problem with Jesus being the way, the truth and the life. The part that people have a problem with is what follows... "no one comes to the father except through me."

Is Jesus the only way to God? The biggest vocalized disagreement with Christianity is "Jesus and Christianity are fine and it is great that you have a way to God. But I have my own way, and the Muslim has his, and the Buddhist has his. All roads lead to God if we are sincere in seeking Him."

That's a fine notion, but that's really all it is. There is no validity to it whatsoever. Why? Check this out: If you consider that Jesus is just a way, then you have to accept the rest of what Jesus said about himself in that same verse, especially the second part... the truth. If you believe that he is "a" way then you have to at least agree that he was an honest man. You can't say, "Well Jesus is a way to God even if he is a total liar." That literally makes no sense whatsoever. You cannot consider Jesus a way to God if at least he isn't an honest man. And if you consider Jesus an honest man, then you have to go back to that first thing he said about himself and realize what this honest man actually said about himself. "I'm not a way, I am the way." There is exclusivity in that statement.

Simply put, if Jesus is not the only way to God, then He is not any way to God. If there are many roads to God, then Jesus is not one of them, because He absolutely claimed there was only one road to God, and He Himself was that road. If Jesus is not the only way to God, then He was not a honest man; He then would either be a madman or a lying devil. There is no middle ground.

If it is all up to personal opinion–if we can determine what Jesus said or didn't say on our own whims–then we can just throw out the gospel altogether. It really is an all-or-nothing deal. Either we take the words of Jesus as recorded by these historically reliable and accurate documents, or we throw it out all together. There is exclusivity in what Jesus said about himself.

Exclusivity of Marriage

This is what people struggle with so much. They struggle with being told "this is the only way." Most every other area of your life you want exclusivity.

For example, 13 years ago my wife and I started dating. We fell in love and we both knew that we wanted to spend the rest of our lives together. The next step was getting engaged. I was super romantic, kneeling down on one knee proposing. She of course said yes. She actually said "Holy crap! Holy crap!" Which translates as "Yes." We went to set the date and she said, "I would like a long engagement, like a year and a half." I said, "I was thinking like 6 weeks." So we compromised and went with a year and a half.

The day of our wedding finally arrived and I was standing in the front waiting for my bride to walk down the aisle. I was looking good. The music played, everyone stood up and there she was... and she was looking hot. I was nudging my best man, "she's mine." The minister started talking and the ceremony was on its way. It was during this ceremony that we committed to being exclusive to each other.

In every ceremony there is a question asked of both the bride and groom and their job is to answer that question with either an "I will" or an "I do." The question goes like this:

(Name of Bride/Groom), will you have this man/ woman to be your husband/wife to live together in the holy covenant of marriage? Will you love, comfort, honor and keep them, in sickness and in health, and, forsaking all others, be faithful to him so long as you both shall live?

At the end of this little question is where you say "I do" or "I will." This is a statement of exclusivity. You are saying, "I am dedicating myself to you, you're the only one for me, I will literally forsake everyone else for you." It's a statement of exclusivity in your marriage and that's exactly what you want.

You don't want to get to that part and have the other person answer that question with "maybe." That throws all exclusivity all out the window. You're saying, "I'm gonna love you and cherish you and honor you but that's it. That whole death till us part thing and faithfulness thing, I don't know about that. But I'm gonna love you and cherish you and honor you but that's it, that's conditional until someone better looking or smarter or richer comes along." If they ever say that in a ceremony, you had better go over, rip that wedding license up and run for your life.

You want your spouse to be exclusive. Guys you don't want your wife telling you "Honey, I'm gonna go hang out with the guys tonight." Oh no you're not. Ladies, in the same way, you don't want your husband telling you "Honey, I'm going to go watch Grey's Anatomy with Sheryl and Belinda." "Oh you're not doing anything with Sheryl and Belinda." You want exclusivity in your marriage.

I want my wife to be exclusively mine. She calls me "babe." That's what my wife calls me. I am exclusively "babe" to my wife. No other guy is "babe" to my wife. That's my title. That's my job. I'm the only "babe" to my wife. Being exclusive makes it that much more meaningful and special.

All Exclusive
But you don't want exclusivity just in your marriage. You want it in other areas too. I am exclusively "dad" to my two sons. My sons will not call any other random dude "dad." That's my title. That's my job. It's special and meaningful and it's mine.

When it comes to that promotion that makes you the regional manager, how would you feel if your boss said to you, "We're promoting you to regional manager... along with all the other employees." Regional manager is a big deal, unless everyone else is the regional manager.

Or in school where you were the only one that studied for the test and you were the only one that actually got that A+. Then the teacher said to you, "Congratulations, since you got an A+, everyone gets an A+!" No, that's not how it's supposed to work. That A+ is exclusively yours; no one else earned it.

Deep down inside, we all want exclusivity in our lives. And the reason for that is this: we all want assurance. **Exclusivity guarantees assurance.**

You want assurance in your marriage. You want assurance in your family. You want assurance in your job. You want assurance in all areas of your life. Don't you want a spiritual assurance as well?

The Reason for the Struggle

Now here's the thing: deep down inside that's exactly what you want. We all want spiritual exclusivity. We want assurance of our relationship with God. Everyone wants that assurance with God.

The reason people struggle with the exclusivity of the gospel is not because of what it Jesus says in John 14:6, but because how loudly Christians proclaim it with the wrong intentions. When Christians proclaim "nobody comes to the father but by me," they're not talking about following Jesus. They're not talking about obeying Jesus. They're certainly not talking about staying faithful under hardship and persecution. No, they're talking about how wrong Muslims, Hindus, Buddhists, Liberal Christians, Humanists, and various other "unbelievers" are. They're usually talking about their certainty that all of the above are destined to burn forever in hell.

I guess that's why I am so amazed by Jesus. Everything about Him is just so right. People don't struggle with the exclusiveness of the Gospel because of Jesus. They struggle with the exclusiveness because of you and me. We're getting in the way of Him. People don't see Jesus because we are in the way.

What?

Which brings me to something else outrageous that Jesus said. This time the outrageous part wasn't said about him, it was said about us. In John 8:12 Jesus said this about himself... "I am the light of the world. Whoever follows me will never walk in darkness, but will have the light of life."

I don't think this is really that outrageous. Honestly, most people would agree with this. Even if people just thought he was a good guy, they would say, "Yep, he's the light of the world." They wouldn't have a problem with this. Jesus is awesome. Jesus is a nice guy. Jesus is holy. Jesus is pure. Jesus is righteous. So most people would have absolutely no problem with this. I have no problem with this. You have no problem with this. Most people don't.

What Jesus said about himself here isn't outrageous. What is outrageous- and some might even consider impossible- is what Jesus said about you and I in **Matthew 5:14**... "You are the light of the world." What!?! Not only does that sound impossible, it actually sounds crazy. I think this is the most outrageous thing Jesus ever said. Jesus claimed that for himself and then he went ahead and said the same thing about you and I. Right now I want you to say that out loud: **I am the light of the word.** Feels weird to say it doesn't it?

Weird and Gross

Here's the reason why I have such a hard time with this. Human beings are weird. We are just plain weird and gross. We do weird things. We say weird things. We do gross things. Humans are just plain weird.

Let me elaborate for a second. Women have this thing that they do where they can have one conversation about five different topics. That's weird to me. I have to take notes when I'm talking with my wife. "So I was at school today, what do you want for dinner tomorrow night, and all of a sudden, don't forget you're picking up Jonas on Wednesday, the bell rings, did you know that Susan and Joe broke up, 5 minutes early, I need to get a haircut." I'm taking notes because one false move and I'm gonna have to recite everything back to her. "Um, you were at school and Jonas rang the bell. While picking up Susan, Joe broke something, oh and we're cutting your hair for dinner tomorrow night." Ladies I know what you would say about that, "We're just so smart we can have one conversation with six topics." I personally think you do it because you forget what your talking about and have to switch topics until you remember. But that's just me. That's weird, but guess what? **"You're the light of the world."**

Or how about this: There is a lot of testosterone running around my house. Between myself, two sons, and a male chihuahua, that's a lot of testosterone. My boys are just weird and gross. For no reason whatsoever- because there can't be a real reason for them to actually do this-my two sons will strip down completely naked and start running around the house. Sometimes they'll do it when we have guests. They will jump out from around corners and go "AHHHHHHH!" completely naked! That's weird, but guess what? **"You're the light of the world."**

Or just guys in general. The grown adult male is by far the poster child for weird and gross. I was listening to the radio the other day and did you know that the average single male only changes his bed sheets four times a year? That's it. Four times a year. Most single females change their sheets every two weeks. Guys are disgusting. We're the same ones that just throw random clothes on the floor when we're finished wearing them. And when we run out of clothes to wear, we turn to the floor. And we all use the same test to determine whether something wearable or not... the sniff test.[83] We will sniff our dirty clothes to determine whether or not they are good enough to wear again. And here is the strangest part: it doesn't even have to pass the sniff test for us to wear it. Why sniff them in the first place? A man will wear dirty clothes for an extended period of time just because they don't want to do laundry. That is disgusting and weird, but guess what? **"You're the light of the world."**

Isn't that weird? Isn't that strange? That's why I think it's the most outrageous thing Jesus has ever said. We aren't holy. We aren't pure. We aren't righteous. Although I think it's strange, I am also excited about this. This gets me pumped up because Jesus honors us by giving us the greatest compliment in the world. He shares His title with us. And we get that title not because we are worthy of it, but because He is worthy of it and we just so happen to be His.

But here is the biggest part of this too, the most exciting part. It is the part that gives you a reason to get out of bed every single day. It's the part that gives you a reason to leave your home. It's the part that gives you a reason you can be excited to go to work or school. Not only is it the greatest compliment he could have ever given us, it's also the greatest purpose he could ever had given us.

Love God, Love Others, Live To Serve

Jesus loved His father. He was given a task to do and his obedience was a show of his love for the father. Jesus loved people. He loved the unloveable. He sat and ate with people no one else would. He healed the sick and cared for the broken. Jesus lived to serve. Paul wrote in Philippians 2 that although Jesus was equal with God, he chose to become a servant to us. I look at that and I think that's a very good definition of being the light of the world.

At our church, we believe that we exist to Love God, Love Others, and Live to Serve. It's not just words. It's not just something easy to remember. It's not just something catchy to repeat... **it's our purpose for existing**. It is us living out what Jesus calls us... the light of the world. We are being the light when we Love God, Love Others and Live to Serve.

This next part of Matthew 5 is my favorite visual... A town built on a hill cannot be hidden. Neither do people light a lamp and put it under a bowl. Instead they put it on its stand, and it gives light to everyone in the house. In the same way, let your light shine before others, that they may see your good deeds and glorify your Father in heaven.[84]

The Night Light

My boys have night-lights in their rooms because they are afraid of the dark. They're actually more of a spotlight than night-lights, but hey, they get the job done. Picture this with me for a second. I'm reading a book to my boys under the light of their night-lights. We finish the book. We pray together. I put them both in their beds and give them hugs and kisses. Then right before I leave, I take a comforter and put it over the light so that it's completely black in their room, turn to them and say "sweet dreams" in a creepy voice and run out of their room. What does that accomplish? It accomplishes two crying and screaming kids. It accomplishes a sure fire way to have my kids sleep in between me and my wife all night long.

If you're going to cover up a light then why have the light in the first place? That's difficult to say, but it's something we truly have to come to grips with... let your light shine before others, that they may see your good deeds and glorify your Father in heaven.

Romans 8:29 teaches us God always intended that we would be like his son. Paul tells the Corinthians church, **1 Corinthians 11:1**, to follow his example as he follows the example of Christ. I want to tell you... that's us. We are the light of this world. Even though we might not be perfect, and we have our faults and our shortcomings, the truth is that every single individual that is in Christ is the light in this dark world. Which means that our everyday life is a reflection of the Father. Our everyday life out there helps people to see God. Our everyday life helps people to draw near to God. Our everyday life is a living example of God's love and His saving grace. That's you. That's us. We are the light of the world.

When we live our life, allowing our light to shine, people will see Jesus. When we give a cold cup of water to someone who is thirsty, people see Jesus. When we give a plate of warm food to someone who is hungry, people see Jesus. When we take time off to go out of the country to help build schools, people see Jesus. When we sacrifice our money to buy water filters for a village where their water is killing them, people see Jesus. When we give school supplies to under-privileged kids, people see Jesus.

Christianity has been called narrow-minded and intolerant. That's what happens when we aren't letting our light be seen. But Biblical Christianity is the most pluralistic and tolerant of all religions. In fact, it is the one religion that has embraced other cultures, and has the most urgency to translate the Scriptures into other languages. A Christian can keep their native language and culture, and follow Jesus in the midst of it. An early criticism of Christianity that they would take anybody! Slave or free, rich or poor. Man or woman. Greek or Barbarian. All were accepted, but on the common ground that Jesus Christ is the way, the truth, and the life.

How Right Jesus Is

Here it is, something that you can never forget: **The gospel isn't about how wrong everyone else is, it's about how right Jesus is.** The gospel of Jesus Christ claims things about him that are true of no one else. Nobody else is Jesus, and no other teaching holds the stunning uniqueness of the One who rose from the dead. As for us, we need to make sure we're not getting in the way of people seeing Jesus. Let your light shine and people will see Jesus.

Jesus gives you exactly what you want and need... exclusiveness that guarantees assurance. Your spiritual destiny is not something you want to take a chance with. You want the right directions. Jesus says "there's no other way than me... I am the way to the father, you can trust me on that one because I'm going to lead you to life."

What do you think?

1. How do you view exclusivity in your marriage? Your job? Your family? Your God?
2. Are you the kind of person that struggles with being told what to do? Why is that?
3. Why do you think so many people would see this as an outrageous or impossible thing to say?
4. How does it make you feel to hear from someone that Jesus is the only way to be with and have a relationship with God? Does your opinion change knowing that Jesus said this?
5. Do you think that people would have a problem with the exclusiveness of the gospel if they could see Jesus through His followers? Why or why not?
6. How can you be the light every day that shows the world God and leads them to Him?

Chapter 7

"SEPARATION ANXIETY"

"Unless there is something to be saved from, there is no point in talking about salvation." –Leon Morris

I don't know if you have noticed this or not, but there are some topics that people just don't want to discuss in church. They're considered too taboo or too controversial for a minister to discuss in front of a group of people. There are things we love to talk about and there are things we can't stand talking about. I have learned that the topics we struggle with talking about are the ones we need to talk more about, not less.

Money

For example, people hate to talk about money in church. There is a certain stigma about money and church. We love to talk about all the different programs and events that the church puts on, but the second a minister starts talking about money, what is the most common thing that will be said, "There the church goes asking for money again!" How do you think the church can afford the programs and events that the congregation readily enjoys? God talked more about money than he did heaven. We love to talk about God forgiving our debt, but we don't want to hear "Don't use credit card because the borrower is slave to the lender." If I refuse to talk about money, then I'm ignoring a lot of what Jesus talked about.

Before I became the lead minister at my church, I was the student minister for 11 years. Prior to the day I stepped into the pulpit, our church hadn't done a series on personal finances and giving for over 8 years. Of course, I felt obligated to do what had been neglected for so long. I did a 5 week study that focused on balancing our personal finances the way God's word had taught us. I don't believe in easing the band-aid off, I believe in ripping it off fast. In week one of our money series, I stood up in front of the congregation and said "Let's talk about money!" As soon as I said that, a guy on the back row got up and walked out. I laughed to myself and just kept going. The good news is that everyone else stayed.[85] We hate to talk about money in the church, which is why we need to talk more about it.

Sex

We also don't like to talk about sex in the church. Why? People think it's dirty and disgusting and has no place in the church. Of course, those are the people that have never studied the Song of Songs, also known as the Song of Solomon. I know this is going to sound extremely weird, but the Song of Songs is the sexiest book in the Bible. We like to talk about being a good husband and a good wife, but we treat this as a separate issue to sex.

Paul calls this a marital duty to being a good husba[nd]
a good wife.[86]

Of course, I felt obligated to preach a series on
sex called "Bringing Sexy Back!" I stood up in front
of the congregation and said "Let's talk about sex!"
Simultaneously, everyone immediately broke eye con-
tact with me. For seven weeks, nothing was too taboo to
talk about in church. I even allowed a time at the end of
each sermon where I would answer anonymous questions
about sex using God's word. It sounded like a good idea
at first, but it soon became a decision I regretted. There
are only so many times a guy can answer a question about
masturbation. I got to the point where I looked at the congregation and said, "This is the deal about masturbation
from here on out, if you can't spell it you can't do it. No
more questions about masturbation." We hate to talk sex
in church, which is why we need to talk more about it.

God's Wrath

What I want to talk about in this chapter is a topic
that many Christians struggle with, but we need to talk
about it. So, let's talk about the wrath of God! People
don't want to talk about wrath. They want to talk about
love. If you talk about wrath, then you have to talk about
judgment. And if you talk about judgment then you have
to talk about Hell. It all goes together.

People don't like to hear about God's wrath because
it seems like it goes against God's love. We object to
the wrath of God because we typically associate it with
human anger and we see it as an outlet for revenge. We
struggle with how God can be a loving God and still pour

97

his wrath against sin. We don't like to talk about it, but you cannot deny it when it comes to God's word.

Wrath in the Old Testament

Go ahead and look almost any where in the Old Testament. In response to sin God releases his wrath-his punishment for sin. **Leviticus 26:28** says, "then in my anger I will be hostile toward you, and I myself will punish you for your sins seven times over." **Deuteronomy 6:15,** "for the LORD your God, who is among you, is a jealous God and his anger will burn against you, and he will destroy you from the face of the land." God's wrath is a reality. Look at **Psalms 89:46**, "How long, O LORD? Will you hide yourself forever? How long will your wrath burn like fire?"

There is no way around it, God's wrath is a reality. What do you think the plagues were? In **Exodus 7:5**, "And the Egyptians will know that I am the LORD when I stretch out my hand against Egypt and bring the Israelites out of it." The Egyptians had "stretched out" their hand of power and authority over the Israelites. They enslaved God's people. So God poured his wrath out against the Egyptians through the ten plagues.

Attack of the Egyptian Gods

When you look at the specific plagues and the "gods" the Egyptians worship you see a very interesting connection. The first plague of turning water into blood was a direct attack on the Egyptian god Hapi, the god of the Nile River. The next plague was frogs. It was an attack on the god of fertility Heka. The third plague was lice, Geb was the god of the earth. God then releases flies throughout

Egypt. Kheper was a god that is pictured with the head of a fly. Next was the death of their livestock. Apis was a bull-deity that was worshiped by the Egyptians. When God struck the Egyptians with boils, it was a direct attack on Thoth, the god of magic and healing, and Isis, the goddess of medicine. When God rained hail down on Egypt, he was attacking their worship of the sky goddess, Nut. God released locusts to destroy the land and crops of Egypt. Seth was the god of crops. When God blotted out the sun and everything went dark, it attacked their chief god, the sun god Ra. The final plague was the death of their firstborn. Pharaoh was considered a god himself. His first born son would become a god after him. God poured out his wrath against the Egyptians for their sins.

God didn't just pour his wrath out against Gentiles in the Old Testament. He dealt with the Israelites as well. Frequently throughout the Old Testament, God would respond with death or exile whenever the Israelites started worshiping other gods and turning their backs on God.

Wrath in the New Testament

Often in the Old Testament, Israelites and Gentiles both experienced the wrath of God. But to isolate God's wrath just to the Old Testament would be a huge mistake. Wrath isn't just an Old Testament thing.

The Old Testament actually makes references to a future wrath. The prophets referred to it as the "day of the Lord." The prophet Joel wrote "The sun will be turned to darkness and the moon to blood before the coming of the great and dreadful day of the LORD."[87] Obadiah wrote "The day of the Lord is near for all nations. As you have one, it will be done to you; your deeds will return upon your own head."[88]

We see this carry over into the New Testament as well. Luke writes in the book of Acts, "The sun will be turned to darkness and the moon to blood before the coming of the great and glorious day of the Lord."[89] Paul teaches us "For you know quite well that the day of the Lord's return will come unexpectedly, like a thief in the night."[90] Peter practically says the exact same thing, "But the day of the Lord will come like a thief. The heavens will disappear with a roar; the elements will be destroyed by fire, and the earth and everything done in it will be laid bare."[91]

There is no way around the wrath of God. We want to talk about God's love and his salvation, but if we ignore the wrath of God, then all those discussions are worthless. Leon Morris writes, "Unless there is something to be saved from, there is no point in talking about salvation."[92] We have to talk about God's wrath. God doesn't leave any room in scripture to ignore His wrath.

God's wrath is just as much one of His attributes as any of the others. A.W. Pink writes:

"Now the wrath of God is as much a Divine perfection as is His faithfulness, power, or mercy. It must be so, for there is no blemish whatever, not the slightest defect in the character of God; yet there would be if 'wrath' were absent from Him!"[93]

"God is Love"

As humans, we don't have the license to define love according to our own standards and sensibilities. We often assume that love means achieving the ultimate happiness for us and everyone around us. If this were love, then yes, wrath would be incompatible with God's love. But Scripture doesn't define God's love in this way. Scripture defines love according to the character of God. God himself defines what love is.

And because God is love, God is everything love is. God defines what love is. God does not have to save everyone for him to show love. Love, in other words, is essentially wrapped up in the character of God. Though God acts in ways that seem unloving by our standards, they are not unloving by his standards—and his standards are the ones that matter.

Our problem is that we try to understand the love of God by itself. We need to understand God's love in light of His other characteristics. In **1 Peter 1:15-16** it says "But just as he who called you is holy, so be holy in all you do; for it is written: "Be holy, because I am holy." In 2 Thessalonians 1:5-7 the author writes... "All this is evidence that God's judgment is right, and as a result you will be counted worthy of the kingdom of God, for which you are suffering. God is just: He will pay back trouble to those who trouble you and give relief to you who are troubled, and to us as well."

Although God is love, He is also holy and just. He also frequently pours out wrath toward sin. In fact, God sometimes withholds certain attributes in order to exercise others. God withholds His wrath to exercise mercy. God withholds justice to pour out His grace. Of course, God could choose to lavish all humanity with His mercy and therefore choose to withhold His wrath toward everyone. But the Bible doesn't support this. God is patient, not wanting anyone to be condemned. That means that he withholds his wrath to exercise mercy, to give us a chance to choose him. But we do know that there will come a time when judgment will come. Does that mean that God isn't love. Does the eventual wrath of God negate his love? Be very careful how you answer.

Parent's Wrath

In our own lives we don't believe this. Do you ever exercise your wrath? Oh, you have wrath. If you were to punish you kid because they did something wrong, does that mean that you don't love them? Let's say that one of your kids is smacking your other kid repeatedly in the face with a rubber snake that was bought from the from Dollar Tree. Does it mean that you don't love them because you took that rubber snake away as a punishment? No, actually the opposite, the kid getting hit in the face feels loved. Let's say that your 16 year old son or daughter comes home at 2am Saturday morning when they were supposed to be home the day before at 10pm. Not to mention that they have alcohol on their breath. Does it mean that you don't love them when you take their car keys away and ground them for a month? No, you love them and you're trying to protect them.

Your kid doesn't feel loved when you're punishing them. You've exercised your wrath. Maybe you raised your voice and really had to chew them out. Maybe you took something away from them that they really love. Maybe, depending on the age, you had to introduce your hand to their butt, which I like to call "the reminder." "Let me give you a reminder why you shouldn't have done that." That's your wrath, and in the midst of your wrath, you kid doesn't feel loved. But the truth it, you do love them. And your wrath expresses that love.

The Wrath of Justin

I have wrath- the wrath of Justin. It's not that impressive. One day, Jonas got in trouble. He's a great kid, but he gets in trouble like any other kid. He loves his little brother, but sometimes he doesn't like him too much. So he'll do somethings to get Toby to leave him alone, such as pushing him down or taking a toy from him. One time, after many, many warnings Jonas got into a bit of trouble. I had to unleash my wrath, aka, timeout. I know that doesn't sound that bad, but for a kid, it's the end of the world. He cried and pouted and he said something that caught my attention. He said, "Why are you being so mean to me?" I responded by laughing. He said the same thing to my wife too. She laughed too.

Once I got my laughter under control I explained to him, "I'm not being mean to you. Actually, I'm loving you by punishing you. I want my son to grow up to be a productive member of the church and society. I don't want my son to grow up to be a jerk." I have to unleash my wrath sometimes to punish him. My wrath doesn't negate my love. It helps to express it.

The same thing goes for God. His wrath doesn't negate his love. While God is love, he is also holy and just, and with sin comes punishment. Scripture says that the penalty of sin is death. We have to understand the love of God in light of his other characteristics. **No other characteristic shows the depth of God's love like his wrath.** Let me explain.

Sin Separates

God hates sin. It goes against everything that He is. When we live the life of a sinner, we are asking to experience God's wrath. That wrath is an eternal separation from God. That wrath makes us unable to be in the presence of the one true God of the entire universe. Isaiah helps us to understand this, "Surely the arm of the Lord is not too short to save, nor his ear too dull to hear. But your iniquities have separated you from your God; your sins have hidden his face from you, so that he will not hear."[94] How does sin separate us from God? It doesn't separate us from His love, we know that God loves sinners. But sin still separates:

"Sin separates us from fellowship with God, because at least at the point of our sin, we no longer think alike with God. Sin separates us from the blessing of God, because at least at the point of our sin, we are not trusting God and relying on Him. Sin separates us from the some of the benefits of God's love, even as the Prodigal Son was still loved by the father, but didn't enjoy the benefits of his love when he was in sin. Sin separates us, in some way, from the protection of God, because He will allow trials to come our way to correct us."[95]

There is still more to this separation though. Paul writes, "They will be punished with everlasting destruction and shut out from the presence of the Lord and from the majesty of his power" [96] In **Daniel 3**, the three Jewish young men were completely comfortable in the fiery furnace, because they weren't alone. The Lord was with them in the fire. The reason Hell is so devastating is because of our separation from God. To be separated from God means to be away from anything good or blessed from the

Lord's presence. "From the presence of the Lord" sums up what God's word says about his wrath.

The Garden

That's why God's wrath helps us to see the true depth of God's love for us. We love to talk about love and salvation but sometimes we fail to grasp the full reality of what God actually did. Paul tells us "Since we have now been justified by his blood, how much more shall we be saved from God's wrath through him!"[97] Jesus didn't just save us from God's wrath- he took God's wrath upon himself.

We know that when Jesus first arrived on the scene to start his public ministry, John the Baptist recognized Him as "the Lamb of God." This title not only means sacrifice, but also that he was going to be the target of God's wrath for the sins of mankind. And Jesus knew this.

The night before Jesus went to the cross, he was kneeling down in a garden praying. When you read the account, you see a very emotional and distraught Jesus. Peter, James, and John were with him and he looked back to them and said "My soul is overwhelmed with sorrow to the point of death. Stay here and keep watch with me."[98] I don't know if you see the emotion that I see, but Jesus has spent three years of his life with these three men. They are friends, and Jesus looked at them and said "Please just stay with me."

He was on the ground, and the prayer just came right out of His mouth, "My Father, if it is possible, may this cup be taken from me. Yet not as I will, but as you will."[99] It was a very passionate prayer that he prayed not just once, but several times. He wanted it another way. He was pleading with God to spare him. And Luke tells us that he was in such "anguish" that he prayed harder and started sweating blood.

Hematridosis

Hematridosis is a very rare condition where the human starts to sweat blood.[100] It occurs when people are suffering from extreme levels of stress. Jesus was about to experience something he had never experienced. And his stress is not over what you would expect. Jesus wasn't sweating blood over the cross. He was sweating blood over his separation from his father.

Separation Anxiety

I need to tell you a secret. You have to promise not to tell anyone. I like to pretend that I am a very manly man that never cries. Honestly, I'm a total softy. In chapter 1, I said that real men don't cry when they watched the movie Titanic, because they didn't watch the movie Titanic. I never watched the Titanic. I reasoned that I already knew the end of the movie, so what was the point? Spoiler Alert: The boat sinks.

I will admit right now, if I watched Titanic today, chances are I will probably cry. My wife and kids have ruined me. I literally cry at everything. In every single Disney movie that I watch with my kids, I'm crying while my kids are going "It's ok daddy." I even cry in action movies. I cried in Transformers. I cried in The Amazing Spider-man. I even cried in Footloose, and it's not even an emotional movie. The only movie I didn't cry in was the one movie that everyone else did cry in: Castaway. When Tom Hanks loses his volley ball, I started laughing out loud in the middle of the movie theater.[101] Pretty much ever other movie I watch, I cry in.

I blame this on my wife and kids. I have what I like to call a separation anxiety. Sometimes, my wife will take the boys to go visit her mom on the weekends. I don't always get to go because I have to be ready for church on Sunday. This means I have to stay home alone. When Fay and the boys leave on a Friday night for the weekend, I always see them off. When they pull out of the driveway I start going through mild depression because I hate to be apart from them. I can't stand the separation.

Preparing for the Separation

That's what Jesus was preparing for in the garden. He was preparing for that separation. He was not in anguish because of the pain he was getting ready to experience. He didn't want to experience the pain just like any one of us wouldn't. But the source of his anguish was not the pain. It wasn't the devastating and brutal torture he was physically getting ready to go through. It's wasn't the cruel cross. None of that was the source. The reason Jesus was so emotionally distraught to the point of sweating blood, was because of what came after all of that. Separation.

Think about it. In the very beginning, Jesus was with God. In the very beginning, Jesus was God. Jesus experienced constant fellowship with his father up until this point. It was the reason he cried out "My God, my God, why have you forsaken me?"[102] This was the point at which Jesus began to experience the separation from his father.

In his book Knowing God, J.I. Packer says this about Jesus taking God's wrath upon himself:

"The wrath of God against us, both present and to come, has been quenched. How was this effected? Through the death of Christ. 'While we were enemies, we were reconciled to God through the death of his Son' (Romans 5:10). The 'blood' — that is, the sacrificial death — of Jesus Christ abolished God's anger against us, and ensured that His treatment of us for ever after would be propitious and favorable. Henceforth, instead of showing Himself to be against us, He would show Himself in our life and experience to be for us. What, then, does the phrase 'a propitiation . . . by His blood' express? It expresses, in the context of Paul's argument, precisely this thought: that by His sacrificial death for our sins Christ pacified the wrath of God."[103]

Jesus accepted the full force of God's wrath for our sake. So many times we flippantly talk about the love of God without realizing just how deep that love actually goes. He accepted separation from the father. He was in the grave for three days. Peter tell us "But do not forget this one thing, dear friends: With the Lord a day is like a thousand years, and a thousand years are like a day."[104] Jesus knew what was coming, but he accepted the wrath that our sins earned. "He is the atoning sacrifice for our sins, and not only for ours but also for the sins of the whole world." [105] The love of God isn't just dying for our sins, but accepting the separation punishment from the father. "He is the atoning sacrifice for our sins, and not only for ours but also for the sins of the whole world."[106]

What better way to see the depth of God's love for us than through his wrath.

Camp Dean

When Jesus takes our deserved wrath, mercy is accessible to all of us. Mercy is a beautiful thing. For five years, I was the dean for the High School week at Lake Aurora Christian Camp. At first, it sounded like a pretty glamorous position. I was the dean of camp. I got my own apartment to sleep in. I also got this little walking talkie that never worked. It was not a glamorous job at all. I spent the majority of the time putting out fires and kicking kids out of camp for breaking the rules. Basically, I was the harbinger of the camp's wrath. And I exercised that wrath quite frequently. Whether it was drugs or alcohol or sex. Unfortunately, I had to dispense that wrath and punish the kids by calling their parents to come and pick them up from the camp they had paid to go to. There were a few times I was able to show mercy, though. It felt good to show mercy. Whenever I got the chance, I would go for it.

Every year I had some helpers from my youth group join me at camp. It was a great deal for them. They got to spend a week at camp for free and had to volunteer in the worship band, running the sound board or media. Anything I needed, they were there to help out with. Of course I took advantage of the situation by making them get me coffee, without the spit. It is very important to order your coffee without spit. I had two rules: 1) Don't date the campers. 2) Don't do anything to get in trouble.

I know the second rule seems very general, but general was extremely important with my youth group. They were always looking for loopholes. I can't tell you how many times I heard things like "I didn't know I wasn't supposed to pour hot soup down the throat of my sleeping roomate!" Or, "I didn't know I wasn't supposed to poop in the tank of the toilet!"[107] So I had to be very general.

One year, I had a group of three young men join me for camp. I went over the rules and said, "If you break the rules, I'll send you home just like I would any other camper." They all agreed and promised to be on their best behavior. Something I have learned about most teenagers is that they are compulsive liars. That promise lasted all of a day. The next day, I got a call from the front desk of the camp that my "volunteers" had a water balloon fight with some campers in one of the dorms. The camp had a policy on water balloons: they're not allowed. So I had to punish them.

It was just some water balloons. It wasn't that big of a deal, but it was a great opportunity to teach a lesson.[108] Word got back to me that they were afraid that I was going to kick them out and that their parents would have to drive two hours to pick them up. I couldn't help myself. I walked in and said three words, "Pack your bags!" Then I walked back out. I wasn't really mad, but they didn't know that. I made them pack all of their stuff up and wait at the door. Thirty minutes later, I walked back in and played my angry camp dean part very well. There were all terrified, and one of my students started to cry.[109] When I was finished with my speech about breaking the rules I asked them "What did I say would happen if you got in trouble?" All three spoke up, "You said you would kick us out." Then I said, "Well, this is called mercy, unpack your bags." Then I turned to the kid crying, called him a "cry baby," and I walked out. There is your lesson on mercy.

We earned wrath. We deserved wrath. Jesus took that wrath upon himself so that we would never have to be apart from the presence of the Lord.

Seems Impossible

It seems impossible that God can exercise his wrath and still be a loving God. But we have learned that nothing is impossible for God. The way man defines love would make wrath an unloving thing. But if God is love, the definition of love is tied to his character. We need to come to grips with his love in light of his wrath.

The crazy thing is this: only God can do the impossible and show the depth of His love through his terrifying wrath. God's wrath reveals how truly amazing He is. The stuff we don't like to talk about: wrath, judgement, and Hell is the backdrop that reveals the amazing grace of the cross. It brings to light how horrible sin is and it magnifies the unconditional love of God. Christ freely chose to take the wrath that I deserve so that I can experience life in the presence of God. With that in mind, how in the world can we keep from singing, crying, and proclaiming his indescribable love?

What do you think?

1. When you were a kid, describe a time when your parents punished you for going against their rules? At the time, how did you feel? How do you feel about it now?

2. What is the first thing that comes to your mind when you hear about God's wrath?

3. Why do you think people struggle talking about God's wrath?
4. How does God's anger originate and reveal itself?
5. How can God be angry and yet loving? Is this a contradiction?
   Read Isaiah 59:1-2 and 2 Thessalonians 1:9
6. How does your description compare to what God's Word says?
7. How does this help you to understand the anguish Jesus was going through in the Garden?
   Read 1 John 4:10 and Romans 5:9
8. It was said "No other characteristic shows the depth of God's love like his wrath." How does Jesus make this true?
9. In light of how Christ does the impossible and saves us from the eternal separation from God, how does this affect your daily life?

Chapter 8

"I HAVE A SUGGESTION!"

"My argument against God was that the universe seemed so cruel and unjust. But how had I got this idea of just and unjust? A man does not call a line crooked unless he has some idea of a straight line. What was I comparing this universe with when I called it unjust?"   *–C.S. Lewis*

I have a young man in my church named Zack. He is an amazing young man. Zack was born with autism and loves to ask questions. Every time I am around Zack he brings a smile to my face. When I see him I go up and give him a huge hug. Although I can kind of tell that he's not too sure he wants to hug me back, he does anyways. He is innocent and eager to learn and talk.

One day, Zack came up to me after a sermon and said "Justin, I have a suggestion."

Anxious to hear his suggestion, I said, "What's up buddy?"

He said, "Why is there so much evil in the world?"

When he said this I thought, "Well this isn't really a suggestion." Instead, he was asking a question that he wanted me to answer. And of course the question is probably one of the deepest questions there is. So I immediately went into teacher mode and began my compelling speech about "Evil in the World." All of the sudden, he stopped me mid sentence and said "Whoa, whoa, whoa, it was just a suggestion, Justin!"

We both went completely silent. I have to admit that it was kind of awkward. I broke the uncomfortable silence and carefully asked if he wanted an answer or not.

He just looked at me, completely confused and smiling and said "I don't know." Then he walked away. Every time I think about that conversation, I laugh. I just can't help myself.

One night I was thinking about what Zack said, and I realized that because of his complete and total innocence, he wasn't asking a question. He was making a suggestion. He was suggesting that someone do something about all the evil in the world. He desperately wants someone to do something. He wanted God to do something about it... and so do you.

The Problem of Evil

Some believe that the problem of evil is a crack in the foundation of Christianity. Greek philosopher Epicurus was the founder of a school of philosophy known as Epicureanism. The purpose of his philosophy was to attain the greatest happiness and to avoid pain. Pleasure is considered good, whereas pain is evil. You can see how Epicurus would struggle with the problem of pain. He argued:

"Is God willing to prevent evil, but not able? Then he is not omnipotent. Is he able, but not willing? Then he is malevolent. Is he both able and willing? Then whence cometh evil? Is he neither able nor willing? Then why call him God?"

What Epicurus attempted to show is that the co-existence of evil with a God who is omnipotent, omniscient and omnibenevolent is either highly unlikely or impossible. This argument sets God up to be either weak or non-existent or evil.

There are many responses to the problem evil from the Christian perspective. The main reasoning that evil exists is because God is concerned with the greater good. That's where "free will" comes into play. God allows evil to exist because he has given us the freedom to chose what we will do. He's not condoning evil, but he allows us to choose whether we will do right or wrong. The reason there is murder, rape and poverty is because we choose to do those things.

God's Response to Evil

That might help to explain why there is evil in the world, but it's not an answer to why something isn't being done about it. The big question is: what is God's response to the problem of evil? We know that nothing is impossible with God. We know that he is all powerful. We know that there is nothing out of his view; he sees and knows everything. We know that he can be everywhere and anywhere all at once. So with all that we know about our God and how he accomplishes what we believe to be impossible, what is God's response to evil?

Jesus

God's response to evil is a two-fold answer. God's ultimate answer to evil is his son Jesus. Scripture teaches us that "He who does what is sinful is of the devil, because the devil has been sinning from the beginning. The reason the Son of God appeared was to destroy the devil's work."[110] John is very clear here with the purpose of Jesus. A few verses back, we are told His purpose is to **"take aways sins."**[111] Then he boldly states that Jesus showed up to destroy the evil work of the Devil. Jesus' purpose is very decisive. He's the wrecking crew. He came to overthrow and destroy evil.

New Bathroom

About five years ago, Fay and I decided that we needed to make an improvement to our house. The master bathroom was anything but a "master." It was the tiniest room in the entire house. Our closet was bigger than the master bathroom. When I took a shower I couldn't turn sideways. All I could do was just stand there and let the water wash over me. I couldn't bend over to wash my feet or my face would be smushed against the tile. I had to be a contortionist to clean my feet. I could only get one arm up to wash my hair. When I got out of the shower I had to step over the toilet. It was a horrible design for a master bathroom. So we decided to cut our closet in half and go into the garage to create a huge walk-in shower, and to move it away from the toilet because that's just disgusting.

The only problem was that I know absolutely nothing about plumbing. The good news is, I do have a father-in-law that is a plumber. So he came down to run the project and tell me what I needed to do. The first thing he told me was to start ripping up the tile. His reason was that it was something I could do on my own before he got there. So I went to the most reliable source I know- Google- to learn how to remove tile. The instructions went like this:

Step 1: Make sure you have your protective goggles and your gloves on.
Step 2: Gently remove grout from around the tile you want to remove with your grout removal tool.
Step 3: Place the chisel at the edge of the tile and tap with a hammer to remove the tile.

My first thought was, "I have to go to Home Depot." So I headed over there and started looking for what I needed. I didn't even know what a grout removal tool was. It turned out to be basically a metal toothbrush. An hour and a half later, I walked out with everything I needed.

Once I got home, I started to follow the steps. I put the protective goggles on. I put my protective gloves on. I got my grout removal tool out and started going to work. The funny thing is, the entire time I was working, I was thinking "Why do I even need these protective goggles? Is it for dust? Do I not want to get dust in my eyes? Is it that bad?" I was thinking this the entire time I was tapping away at this one tile.

An hour and a half later my father-in-law showed up and I had one tile removed. That's it. It was going a lot slower than I had anticipated. Apparently, it was going a lot slower than my father-in-law anticipated too. He was staring at my one removed tile with this look on his face that said "What in the world are you doing?" Of course, he was very sensitive of my feelings so he didn't say anything mean. He just said "Can I borrow your hammer and protective goggles?" I handed him both, he put the goggles on, and started beating the wall with the hammer like it had just broken into his house. Tile shrapnel was flying at my face, I knew what the goggles were for now. My father-in-law is a lot smaller than me. I'm this big guy that can only get one tile that is the span of my hand out in an hour and a half. He swung the hammer ten times and a third of the tile was already gone. He handed me the hammer and goggles back and said, "Tear it up!"

I took my turn again and I started to beat this wall like it had just stolen my wallet. I tore into this wall like it had been flirting with my wife. I felt angry at this wall. I was yelling at it, "I haven't washed my feet in three years, this is what you get!" Thirty minutes later, I dropped the hammer on the ground and said, "Done!" Then I walked out victorious.

The picture in my mind was that when I removed all the tile, I was going to stack it in a nice and neat little pile. That wasn't my job. My job was to destroy the old bathroom. And that's what I did. I literally demolished the old bathroom; there was nothing left of it when I was done.

His Ultimate Response

Jesus is God's ultimate response to evil. Jesus came to demolish evil; that was his job. He accomplished this through the cross. The author of Hebrews says this about Jesus:

"Since the children have flesh and blood, he too shared in their humanity so that by his death he might destroy him who holds the power of death—that is, the devil—and free those who all their lives were held in slavery by their fear of death."[112]

In the gospel of Luke, we find a group of shepherds gathered in a field for the night. As they watched over the flock, an angel suddenly appeared to them. This terrified them. Shepherds didn't always have the best reputations. They hung out with sheep all day. They smelled bad and didn't have the greatest manners. When an angel showed up, they were not excited, they were scared. The angel calmed their nerves by saying:

"Do not be afraid. I bring you good news of great joy that will be for all the people. Today in the town of David a Savior has been born to you; he is Christ the Lord."[113]

The angel's proclamation served as the beginning of the end. His message was the answer to evil. Jesus had always been God's answer. In Genesis God said, "And I will put enmity between you and the woman, and between your offspring and hers; he will crush your head, and you will strike his heel."[114] This was God's way of say "In the beginning, it was 'game over'." Because of the work that Jesus did on the earth, the end had already been written. Evil loses. God is victorious. Jesus is His ultimate response to the evil in the world.

The Church

But God has another response to evil that we regularly neglect—us. God intends that His Church be the answer evil. In Roman 12, we are taught how we are called to respond to the evil in the world and in our lives. It is a call for harmony and peace. We are told not to seek revenge. Let God take care of that with his wrath. Then Paul quoted a very interesting Psalm:

"If your enemy is hungry, feed him; if he is thirsty, give him something to drink. In doing this, you will heap burning coals on his head."[115]

What in the world does "heap burning coals on his head" mean? It doesn't sound like anything good. Sounds kind of like revenge. When you first read, it sounds like we are supposed to lure them in with our kindness only to unleash our wrath and burn them to death. Actually, it's a very interesting figure of speech. Many commentators understand it as a negative response to evil, a picture of the fires of hell. I don't believe that's where Paul was going with the "burning coals."

What purpose would burning coals have in a home? Is it for punishment? Is it for destruction? Is it to produce pain? No. A wise man would use "burning coals" in his home in order to warm it. In ancient times they kept the fire constantly going in order to cook food and provide warmth. If the fire ever went out, a neighbor would give coals from their fire to help restart it. When the neighbor was exceptionally generous, they would give them plenty of hot coals to help.

When Paul said to give an enemy a drink and some food, that we will heap burning coals on them is actually a good thing. It's not a picture of death or wrath, it's actually a picture of life and even salvation. The last verse in that chapter confirms it:

"Do not be overcome by evil, but overcome evil with good."[116]

Doing Nothing

Edmond Burke said it best: *"All that is necessary for the triumph of evil is that good men do nothing."* When good men do nothing, nothing good get's done. God created each and everyone of us to accomplish good works.

"For we are God's workmanship, created in Christ Jesus to do good works, which God prepared in advance for us to do."[117]

"But love your enemies, do good to them, and lend to them without expecting to get anything back. Then your reward will be great, and you will be sons of the Most High, because he is kind to the ungrateful and wicked."[118]

God always intended for His Church to be the answer to the problem of evil. But when the church does nothing, we are allowing evil to run rampant. Many Christians sit around and say "Why is there so much evil in the world? Why is there murder? Why is there rape? Why is there abortion? Why is there poverty? Why are children all over the world starving to death? Why are people throwing their lives away by killing themselves and others?" **When the good Church does nothing, nothing good gets done.** I don't think many of us know that we are the answer. And those of us that do realize it constantly come up with excuses.

Mean at the Gym

I'm great at coming up with excuses. I am a professional excuse maker. One day I got done at the gym and followed that up with a wonderful dinner choice: Pizza Hut. That's the reason we exercise; to eat pizza. So there I was waiting for my Meat Lovers Pan Pizza and I was talking with one of the employees that I know. We were joking around and laughing. He gave me my pizza and I went home and ate a week's worth of calories in one sitting.

A couple of days later I saw my Pizza Hut friend and he told me that one of his co-workers saw me at the gym all of the time and is scared of me. What? They said that I look mean when I at the gym. He went on to explain to his co-worker that I'm actually a really nice guy.

So what's my excuse? Why don't I smile at the gym? Because deep down I don't like the gym. I like it because it helps to keep me healthy. But at my core, I hate the gym. I reasoned that it's hard to look happy when you have a couple of hundred pounds sitting on your chest. I reasoned that it's hard to look happy when you feel like your arms are going to fall off. I reasoned that it's hard to look happy when you're doing cardio for forty-five minutes and your ankles are so swollen that all you want to do is curl up on the gym floor and go to sleep. That was my excuse. And it's a good excuse, because it is hard to look happy doing all of that. But that's all it is–an excuse. I can look happy doing anything because all I have to think about is how much my God has done for me. It's not impossible, it's just an excuse.

Our Excuses

We do the same thing in our church. We come up with all kinds of excuses in order to do nothing. I'm too young. I'm too old. I'm too inexperienced. I'm too poor. I'm too scared. I'm too... STOP! You're the Church! There is no excuse you can come up with that will ever make sense.

The parable of the talents is about a man that did nothing. The other two servants invested what their master had entrusted them with. They did something good with what they were given. Notice that the one servant didn't do something evil, such as stealing the money. He did nothing and got nothing good done. Instead he came up with an excuse, so the master condemned him.

Jesus saw a fig tree that had no figs on it. He cursed the tree and it withered away and died. Why? Because it did nothing.

Jesus rebuked the church in Laodicea for doing nothing. They weren't "hot or cold." He called them lukewarm. They were a church of spectators. They did nothing and Jesus said "I'll vomit you out of my mouth."

There are no positions in the church called "spectator." The more spectators a church has, the weaker it becomes. The weaker the church becomes, the more evil grows and flourishes. The more that evil grows and flourishes, the more spectator Christians sit around saying "someone should do something about this."

Self-Serve Christianity

When we become spectators in the church, we are prescribing to a self-serve Christianity. As a kid, I remember being in the car with my step-dad and the worse thing in the world would happen... we would have to go get gas. The reason I say it was the worse thing in the world was because as soon as we got to the pump my dad would start his tirade on the cost of gas. It always seemed like a shock to him, as if he didn't just get gas the week before and it was the same price.

"Two dollars for a gallon of gas! This is highway robbery! I remember when gas cost a nickel a gallon! You could fill your tank up for under a dollar! And what's with this whole self-serve business! I remember when it was a nickel a gallon and you didn't even have to get out of your car. Someone would come out and pump your gas for you!"

I like to joke about my dad and his ranting, but I know I'm gonna do the same thing with my boys.

"Eight dollars for a gallon of gas! This is highway robbery! I remember when gas cost four dollars a gallon! You could fill your whole tank up for $50. And what's with this whole "refine your own gas" business! I remember when it was four dollars a gallon and the gas was already refined!"

The point is that in many ways the church has turned into a self-serve church. It's all about "me" and what can the church do to entertain "me" and serve "me." That's why evil thrives. The early church wasn't like this at all. The early church understood what God established them to do; that their purpose was to actively oppose evil.

"Anyone in Need"

The book of Acts teaches us how the early church existed. In chapter two, we see Peter, a fisherman, stand up and deliver the first Christian sermon. In front of thousands of people he said "Repent and be baptized everyone of you." And they do exactly that. Then we have a beautiful description of how the church moved forward:

"They devoted themselves to the apostles' teaching and to fellowship, to the breaking of bread and to prayer. Everyone was filled with awe at the many wonders and signs performed by the apostles. All the believers were together and had everything in common. They sold property and possessions to give to anyone who had need. Every day they continued to meet together in the temple courts. They broke bread in their homes and ate together with glad and sincere hearts, praising God and enjoying the favor of all the people. And the Lord added to their number daily those who were being save."[119]

Did you notice the verse about the early church's tremendous growth? They gave "to anyone in need." The Jews were known for their hospitality during the major feasts. Visitors were received into homes and no one would charge for anything. All of their basic daily needs were provided for. The Christians took this feast-time hospitality and made it an everyday thing. Jesus had become more important than possessions and so had others. They gave to "anyone in need." The early church was not a self serve church. The early church was all about others.

Jesus told the disciples that by their love for each other, the whole world would take notice. Tertullian reported that the Romans would exclaim, "See how they love one another!" Justyn Martyr noticed their love as sacrificial, "We who used to value the acquisition of wealth and possessions more than anything else now bring what we have into a common fund and share it with anyone who needs it." Clement said, "He impoverishes himself out of love."

Plague Love

It wasn't just inside the church either. In the fourteenth century a plague started to spread across the ancient world. It was known as the Black Plague, or the Black Death. Christian rushed to the aid of those that were sick. When you contracted the Black Death it was very painful road to death. It started with tumors the size of apples spreading all over your body. This would be followed by a fever and vomiting blood. Most people died between 2 and 7 days after being infected. The world didn't know what to do with the infected. Families would throw their own family members out on the street in order to protect themselves. The only ones who cared for the sick were the Christians. They took the risk of contracting the disease themselves by loving the infected.

Christians lovingly helped non-believers: the poor, the orphans, the elderly, the sick—even their persecutors. Christians would pull the abandoned, unwanted babies and elderly people out of the woods where it was common to dump them.

Things Are Changing Again

This is how the early church started off. For a long time, however, the church started to become consumers rather than givers. Things are changing again. The church is starting to change again. The church is starting to recognize it's purpose all over again. It's starting to realize the call to love God with everything you have and the call to love other as well. The poor, the orphans, the elderly, the sick—and the persecuted are being served again.

Our church has caught this vision. It's not just about us. We provide backpacks and school supplies to the kids whose families can't afford it. We even get the kids free haircuts to get before school starts again. We help to refill our local food pantry in order to help take care of our community. We go overseas to the mission field to provide clean water to families that could potentially die simple from drinking contaminated water. Every Saturday night we feed the homeless in our community.

I'm proud to say that God is moving through our faith family in a very powerful way. But not just us, the Church all over the world is starting to abandon the self-serve church mentality and starting to be what God had always intended them to be. And when the church does this, evil has no chance.

What is God doing about the problem of evil? Jesus is God's ultimate response to the problem of evil. He has already destroyed the work of the devil. The end has already been written... we win. His church is the second part of His response. That's why it's so important that we all do our part. If you believe that your church can survive with you on the sideline, then you are crippling your church. Paul teaches us that it's about all of us working together:

"We are to grow up in every way into him who is the head, into Christ, from whom the whole body, joined and held together by every joint with which it is equipped, when each part is working properly, makes the body grow so that it builds itself up in love."[120]

When "each part is working properly" then evil doesn't stand a chance. When "each part is working properly" the gospel is shared and disciples are made. When "each part is working properly" needs are met and lives are changed.

Is the impossible God willing to prevent evil? Yes. Is the impossible God able? Yes. And his response to the evil that man does is His son and His Church.

What do you think?

1. What does "free" mean?
2. Let's assume that one day scientists will be able to create "intelligent computers" which can make their own choices with their free will. Should one

of the computers make an error, who will you hold responsible for that error? If you hold the scientist responsible, won't you be contradicting your previous acceptance that computers have free will?

3. How would you describe, in your own words, what the classical "problem of evil" is?

4. Why do you think that the the co-existence of God and evil is always referred to as a problem?

5. Which side of the apparent contradiction does your proposed answer change
   Read 1 John 3:5-8 & Hebrews 2:14-15

6. According to verse 8, why did Jesus appear?

7. How does Jesus decisively deal with the work of the devil?

8. How is this God's response to the "problem of evil?"
   Read Romans 12:20-21 & Psalm 25:21-22

9. What is the first thing that comes to your mind when you read about the "burning coals?"

10. How does Paul say the Christian should relate to the non-Christian?

11. How does the church continue to ride the wave of Christ' finished work against evil?

12. Describe one way that you can actively oppose the evil that man does in this world as an individual? As the Church?

Chapter 9

"STATUE ERECTION"

"Do you wish to rise? Begin by descending. You plan a tower that will pierce the clouds? Lay first the foundation of humility."   *–Augustine*

Humility is something I struggle with. Not being humiliated. I believe this book has proven that I have no problem with being humiliated. I think of it as an occupational hazard. When I say that I struggle with humility, I mean that I think way too highly of myself.

I know I'm not the only one either. Most of us tend to think way too much of ourselves. I want to tell you what is foundational to understanding the Impossible One and yourself in light of Him. **Healthy humility**, which means, less of me and more of him.

This healthy humility is exactly what Nebuchadnezzar needed and got. In **Daniel 3** we see the King of Babylon, Nebuchadnezzar made an image of gold that was 90 feet tall and 9 feet wide and he commanded that everyone bow down and worship it. It takes a huge ego to do something like that.

Monument to Self

I want to take a survey real quick, how many of you reading right now have erected a monument to yourself? No, seriously, think about it for a second. In your front yard is there a statue dedicated to yourself where people could come and check it out and pay homage to it, perhaps bow down to it? The answer is more than likely no. If the answer is yes then you probably need to put this book down, go outside, and tear down your "Temple to Joe."

Chances are, none of you have a shrine dedicated to yourself in your front yard. That would be ridiculous and absurd. People would drive by and throw things at it. Every night it would be toilet papered.[121] You're just asking for people to mess with you.

Well, Nebuchadnezzar built a ninety foot statue. It was not necessarily a statue of himself, although it could have been. Even if it wasn't, it might as well been have with the ego that Nebuchadnezzar had. In Daniel 4, the king had a dream that needed to be interpreted:

"'This is what the dream means, Your Majesty, and what the Most High has declared will happen to my lord the king. You will be driven from human society, and you will live in the fields with the wild animals. You will eat grass like a cow, and you will be drenched with the dew of heaven. Seven periods of time will pass while you live this way, until you learn that the Most High rules over the kingdoms of the world and gives them to anyone he chooses. But the stump and roots of the tree were left in the ground. This means that you will receive your kingdom back again when you have learned that heaven rules. "'King Nebuchadnezzar, please accept my advice.'"[122]

Daniel said "Lose the ego. Take my advice and stop sinning. Learn now or else." Twelve months later, everything that Daniel said happened. As Nebuchadnezzar was strolling along looking at his kingdom from his palace he said this (here's that ego I'm talking about):

he said, "Is not this the great Babylon I have built as the royal residence, by my mighty power and for the glory of my majesty?"[123]

Scripture says that the words were still on his lips when immediately he found himself somewhere else and everything that Daniel told was being fulfilled. The author of Proverbs writes... "He mocks proud mockers but gives grace to the humble."[124]

This was the lesson that Nebachadnezzar needed to learn and it's the same lesson that we need to learn as well. James and Peter both referenced this verse. Paul taught the same thing. This is a common thread woven throughout scripture: God will humble the proud.

The Polish Effect

What we need is a **Copernican Revolution**. Polish astronomer Nicholas Copernicus challenged scientific and religious thought about 500 years ago. He suggesting that the earth actually revolved around the sun, not the other way around.

Many of us live as if everything is about us. It's the plague of our society. We are selfish and ego driven. Everything is about us and the world caters to that thought pattern. Why do you think there are so many industries out there that are dedicated to making you feel special. If you don't like the way you look, change your face. If you lose your hair earlier than you expect, just get some more "plugged" in. Maybe you have more hair on your body than you signed up for, that's ok, get it removed via laser.[125] If you're not happy with your bust line, just make it bigger. Everywhere you look you'll see more and more products designed to feed you ego and make you feel special. Supply is high because demand is higher.

We are full of pride, and pride is the root of every other sin. Pride is when we worship ourselves above God. It's the root of every other sin. It's what caused Adam and Eve to fall. The temptation was to be like God. Eat the fruit that God said not to and you will be like God. Eat the fruit and you will be worthy of worship. Pride happens when we tell God that we refuse to center our life around Him.

What If?

In our solar system, planet earth revolves around a huge fire ball known as the sun. Have you ever thought about what would happen if the earth suddenly stopped revolving around the sun? If this were to ever happen, the results would be catastrophic. What would happen? The answer is complete geographic reformation. Gravity would pull the oceans towards the poles creating new land masses. Some scientist even believe that it would affect the integrity of the earth, meaning that it would shake and shift constantly if it didn't revolve around the sun. Say goodbye to seasons. Days would cease to exist as we know them. One side would exist in a perpetual darkness, the other would exist in constant heat of the sun. Plants would start to wither and die. Animals that feed on plants would start to starve to death. The carnivores that depend on those animals would start to starve to death... Including us. That's what would happen if the earth stop revolving around the sun. The next question that needs to be asked is: What if the sun ceases to exist? What if it disappeared?

If the sun mysteriously turned off or disappeared, we would be in big trouble. Within a week the average surface temperature would drop to 0° F. Within a year, it would drop to -100° F. The surface of the sea would freeze over. The temperature would bottom out at -400° F. But we would never see that. We would last a very short time in a post-sun existence.

Of course, the sun doesn't merely heat the Earth. It also keeps the planet in orbit. If its mass suddenly disappeared, the planet would fly off, like a ball swung on a string and suddenly let go. If the sun burned out or disappeared then the result would be Chaos... Disaster... Death. The same thing happens when we try to steal God's glory... disaster.

Copernicus had a theory "The earth revolves around the sun." He was right. God is challenging us in the same way.

"I am the Impossible One. You revolve around me."

Get Married

Get married and you will realize what God wants. It's not you exclusively, it's 'us'. You cannot be happily married and be selfish at the same time. I don't know a single couple that is happily married and the husband or wife are selfish. They might not be divorced, but they definitely aren't happy. Take it one step further. Have kids and you'll realize what God wants. There is no room for selfishness when kids are in the picture. You share everything. You share your food. You share your drinks. You share your bed. I can't tell you how many times I have woken up in the middle of the night with a toddler's foot kicking me in the face. Selfishness is what God is trying to remove from our lives. G.K. Chesterton, **"How much happier you would be, how much more of you there would be if the hammer of a higher God could smash your small cosmos."**

One moment, Nebachadnezzar was in his palace admiring all that he had done. And the next...

"Nebuchadnezzar was driven from human society. He ate grass like a cow, and he was drenched with the dew of heaven. He lived this way until his hair was as long as eagles' feathers and his nails were like birds' claws."[126]

That is what happens when God smashes your cosmos. **There comes a point in your life where you get to the end of yourself,** where everything is stripped away. It's in that moment when you realize that God is God and that's all you need. Let that moment be right now for you:

[34] "After this time had passed, I, Nebuchadnezzar, looked up to heaven. My sanity returned, and I praised and worshiped the Most High and honored the one who lives forever... [36] "When my sanity returned to me, so did my honor and glory and kingdom. My advisers and nobles sought me out, and I was restored as head of my kingdom, with even greater honor than before. [37] "Now I, Nebuchadnezzar, praise and glorify and honor the King

of heaven. All his acts are just and true, and he is able to humble the proud."[127]

Nebuchadnezzar had this **Copernican Revelation** and came to this conclusion about God: "If I try to exalt myself, God will find a way to humble me." But here is the flip side to this relationship with God: When we humble ourselves, worship and serve God, then God will exalt you.

James reminds us **"Humble yourselves before the Lord, and he will lift you up."**[128] It all comes down to this, God is God and we are not. He is the Impossible One and we are his creation. If you want to know the one that heals the blind and brings the dead back to life... then humble yourself. If you want to know the one that spoke creation into existence... then humble yourself. If you want to truly know the one that saves... then humble yourself. If you want to know the Impossible One... then humble yourself.

What do you think?

1. So, what do you think about the Impossible God? Are you ready to take the next step? I encourage you to find a local church or talk to a friend who is already a follower of Christ to help guide you on your journey.

ENDNOTES

1 One of my friends said the key to being a real man is "a good woman." Wrong answer! He is now just an acquaintance.

2 My student minister Eli Robinson struggles with the bar. Apparently he also gets "Tennis Elbow" from moving a rather light couch. I thought you had to play tennis to get tennis elbow.

3 Same goes for proper grammar; when I wrote this the first time I spelled 'grammar' wrong.

4 By "Air Supply" I am referring to both the actually breath of life and the band. Yes, I just did a shout out to Graham Russell and Russell Hitchcok.

5 Except for my friend Mike Hoornstra. The rumor is that the only hair on his body is on the top of his head and that poor imitation of a Zorro mustache he has.

6 The only exception was when Eli Robinson was playing golf with our friend Chris Maiden. One time Chris hit Eli on the left butt cheek with a golf ball. Now golf is always stressful for Eli, especially when Chris is playing too. It left a rather large bruise. I have a picture of it but since

this is a Christian book, I can't show you. I can however text it to you. Hit me up.

7 I hesitated to use this one day in a sermon because my mom was in attendance. Then, my better judgment prevailed and I used it anyways. She loved it.

8 I have to take a moment to explain this. The RKO is the finishing move of WWE wrestler Randy Orton. The move consists of jumping in the air while holding someone's head over your shoulder and then slamming their face into the mat. Randy Orton is my best friend Dana's favorite wrestler. He's the 125 lb. guy that's going to RKO you.

9 1 John 3:20

10 Psalm 139:7-8

11 Jeremiah 32:17

12 Johnson University Florida

13 www.godisimaginary.com

14 www.godisimaginary.com

15 Luke 1:30-33

16 Luke 1:35-37

17 James 1:26

18 1 Peter 3:10

19 1 Peter 3:10

20 When I impersonate my mom I make her sound like either Katherine Hepburn or Joan Rivers.

21 Genesis 1:1-2

22 1 Kings 19:3-5

23 Guzik, David. "Study Guide for 1 Kings 19." Blue Letter Bible. Sowing Circle. 7 Jul, 2006. Web. 26 Sep, 2013. <http://www.blueletterbible.org/Comm/guzik_david/StudyGuide_1Ki/1Ki_19.cfm>.

24 1 Kings 19:9

25 1 Corinthians 1:3-4

26 Psalm 34:18

27 1 Kings 19:14

28 1 Kings 19:15-18

29 The really hard theological question this brings up is, did he know he was going to trip in the first place? And if he did know, why did he still trip? I'm sorry, I just couldn't help myself.

30 www.kidstalkaboutgod.org

31 1 Timothy 3:16

32 That's not an exact quote. It is a rather accurate description of what they meant and actually what all college students mean when they say "lets go get something to drink." They're basically saying "Let's drink until we get alcohol poison."

33 It has come to my attention that not everyone knows what a "taquito" is. They're really nothing to write about. Which is why I chose to write about them. They are basically a rolled up taco. Sounds great. They're not.

34 I always had a horrible haircut and my hair always hung in my eyes. When I did get my hair cut it looked like someone started cutting my bangs, got bored and just quit.

35 Yeah, I'm bitter. But writing this out has been very therapeutic for me. I can finally let it go.

36 My mom didn't think this was very funny at all.

37 Every time I get a picture for my license or my passport they always yell at me "don't smile, just look natural!" Well apparently when I look natural I look like an angry terrorist. Never fails.

38 Matthew 11:3

39 Matthew 11:4-5

40 Matthew 11:25-26

41 I also encourage it because it's a very simple book to read. I read the entire book while going to the bathroom. Not in one sitting, that would be ridiculous. In the span of a week. You could say that McDowell helped me to understand what it means to come to the throne of God while on a throne of my own.

42 John 14:7-10

43 John 10:30

44 Matthew 27:43

45 McDowell, Josh D.; Sean McDowell (2011-08-17). More Than a Carpenter (Kindle Locations 460-462). Tyndale House Publishers. Kindle Edition.

46 Am I supposed to site something like thing and if so how do I go about doing it? Pei Wei, Fortune Cookie?

47 Proverbs 26:11

48 He didn't get in that much trouble honestly. Not as much trouble as his little brother did when he hit the TV with a fishing pole and cracked the LCD screen. How did I respond you ask? By not buying a new TV for 2 months. All my kids kept asking was "can we get a new TV yet?" My answer, "Not until you understand that you are never allowed to touch the TV."

49 Romans 7:14-20

50 2 Corinthians 12:7

51 Romans 7:24-25

52 Isaiah 53:9

53 1 Peter 2:22

54 Hebrews 7:26

55 Matthew 4:2-3

56 Matthew 4:4, Deuteronomy 8:4

57 Psalm 91:11,12

58 Matthew 4:7, Deuteronomy 6:16

59 Matthew 4:10, Deuteronomy 6:13

60 Hebrews 9:22

61 Genesis 4:3

62 Genesis 4:4-5

63 Genesis 8:20-21

64 Some people struggle with this because they think "what in the world did the animal do to deserve this?" Well that's kind of the point, there is an innocence to them that would provide "temporary" forgiveness. But animal rights activist struggle with this. It's why many are vegetarians or vegans. I'm kind of like a vegan, I only eat animals that eat grass. That was meant to be a joke.

65 John 1:29

66 2 Corinthians 5:21

67 1 Corinthians 15:34

68 Or maybe you are like me and you have a lazy eye. My right eye doesn't open all the way. My entire life I have been accused of being high (on drugs). One time I finished preaching a sermon and woman walked up to me and said "Are you high? You look high." This is my face, this is what I look like.

69 Genesis 1:27

70 1 Kings 18:22-26

71 1 Kings 18:27

72 Jonah 1:17

73 Jonah 2:10

74 Mark 4:38

75 Mark 4:38

76 1 Samuel 5:9

77 John 10:10

78 Hebrews 11:25

79 Praise God!

80 Interesting little fact: When my Student minister was looking to get an engagement ring for girlfriend. He asked me to go along. He paid cash for the ring but was short by 14 cents. Good thing I was there, because I am now a share owner in his marriage. I tried to trade it back to him during his wedding in exchange for the right so name his first born child. He refused. Too bad. I was looking forward to meeting Chalupa Batman Robinson.

81 John 14:5

82 John 14:6

83 If this illustration has offended you in anyway please forgive me. I would just like to add however... sometimes the truth hurts.

84 Matthew 5:15-16

85 A guy walked out grumbling under his breath. I can't make this stuff up.

86 1 Corinthians 7:2-5

87 Joel 2:31

88 Obadiah 15

89 Acts 2:20

90 1 Thessalonians 5:2

91 2 Peter 3:10

92 Guzik, David. "Study Guide for Romans 1." Enduring Word. Blue Letter Bible. 7 Jul 2006. 2013. 5 Feb 2013.

93 A. W. Pink, The Attributes of God, (Swengel Pa.: Reiner Publications, 1968 [Reprint]), p. 76.

94 Isaiah 59:1-2

95 Guzik, David. "Study Guide for Isaiah 59." Enduring Word. Blue Letter Bible. 7 Jul 2006. 2013. 6 Feb 2013.

96 2 Thessalonians 1:9

97 Romans 5:9

98 Matthew 26:38

99 Matthew 26:39

100 Holoubek, JE; Holoubek AB (1996). "Blood, sweat and fear. "A classification of hematidrosis"". Journal of Medicine 27 (3–4): 115–33. PMID 8982961

101 So did my wife. What can I say, we were made for each other.

102 Matthew 27:46

103 J. I. Packer, Knowing God (Downers Grove, Illinois: Inter-Varsity Press, 1973), p. 165

104 2 Peter 3:8

105 1 John 2:2

106 1 John 4:10

107 One day I'm going to write a book about all the stupid things my youth group did over the years.

108 And of course mess with them a bit.

109 His name was Jared Beekman. He cried like a little baby. Don't feel bad for him. He deserved it. Plus I get to make fun of him to this day because of it.

110 1 John 3:8

111 1 John 3:5

112 Hebrews 2:14-15

113 Luke 2:11-12

114 Genesis 3:15

115 Romans 12:20; Psalm 25:21-22

116 Romans 12:21

117 Ephesians 2:10

118 Luke 6:35

119 Acts 2:43-47

120 Eph. 4:15–16

121 I would let my dog pee on the foot of your statue. Take that!

122 Daniel 4:24-27

123 Daniel 4:30
124 Proverbs 3:34
125 Ouch!
126 Daniel 4:33
127 Daniel 4:34-37
128 James 4:10